BIOGRAPHY
VILLA

WITHDRAWN

Keeping

3526
9411

D0312445

CARSON CITY LIBRARY
900 N. ROOP STREET
CARSON CITY, NV 89701

WITHDRAWN

Pancho Villa

Strong Man of the Revolution

by

Larry A. Harris

~ ~ ~ ~ ~ ~ ~ ~ ~ ~ ~ ~ ~ ~ ~

Originally published as *Pancho Villa and the Columbus Raid*, 1949,
The McMath Company, Inc. El Paso, Texas.
Library of Congress Catalog Card Number: 49-48005
ISBN: 0-944383-31-9

Introduction copyright 1989 by Andrew Gulliford

~ ~ ~ ~ ~ ~ ~ ~ ~ ~ ~ ~ ~ ~ ~

Second Reprinting (1995) by

High-Lonesome Books
P. O. Box 878
Silver City, New Mexico
88062

Villa as prisoner of General Huerta, 1912.

Pancho Villa's Place in History
an introductory essay to
Pancho Villa: Strong Man of the Revolution

essay by Andrew Gulliford, Ph.D.
Director of the Museum
Middle Tennessee State University
Murfreesboro, Tennessee

Pancho Villa was many men - renowned lover, bandit, horse thief, cattle rustler, revolutionary, murderer, and general. Villa embraced life fully, and rose from humble birth as a Mexican *peon* to become "the strong man of the revolution." Villa is the only guerilla leader whose troops have invaded United States soil in the twentieth century. His name has passed into Mexican folklore, and he is the object of frequent *corridos*, or folk songs and *cuentos*, or folk tales, which enlarge and expand upon his exploits. More crimes have been attributed to Villa the bandit than he could possibly have committed.[1]

Tales of Villa's life and assassination continue to interest professional and amateur historians as well as folklorists. His armed men rode unchecked in Chihuahua, Coahuila, Durango, and Sonora, and his name has become synonymous with the Mexican Revolution. Though a younger generation of Mexican-Americans may think Villa was "bought off" for accepting the 25,000 acre estate deeded to him in 1921 by the Huerta regime, quite possibly it was Adolfo De La Huerta's men who had him killed. Giving Villa the estate may only have been a ruse to placate him to lower his guard. Certainly, the bullets which riddled his car on that fateful day in 1923 were issued by the Mexican government. Like so many of his *compañeros* in *la revolución*, Pancho Villa died at the hands of assassins.

This book was written by Larry A. Harris in 1949 and published in El Paso, Texas, under the title of *Pancho Villa and the Columbus Raid*. Harris describes Villa's life from the perspective of a newsman who meticulously combed back issues of the *El Paso Times* and researched stories and tales of Villa for twenty-two years to assemble this unique version of the Villa legend. There is hyperbole in Harris's description of

i

Villa's exploits, and select passages have a purple tinge to their prose, but there is no discounting Pancho Villa's importance as an historical figure. He was one of the main leaders of the Mexican Revolution, and any analysis of Latin American history must include Villa's meteoric rise from farm laborer to revolutionary general courted by statesmen, diplomats, and foreign powers, particularly the Kaiser's Germany.

Writer and reporter Jim Reed knew Villa well. The only American buried in the Kremlin's Red Square, Reed was sympathetic to the Revolution. In his book *Insurgent Mexico* (1914), Reed describes the Villa of song and legend who, "in time of famine fed whole districts, and took care of entire villages evicted by the soldiers under Porfirio Diaz's outrageous land law . . . [Villa] was the Mexican Robin Hood," who was granted a reprieve only moments before his scheduled execution by a firing squad.[2] John Reed explains that Pancho Villa frequently visited and lived in El Paso "and it was from there that he set out in April, 1913, to conquer Mexico with four companions, three horses, two pounds of sugar and coffee, and a pound of salt."[3]

Villa was a charismatic leader who recruited 10,000 men in five months. In 1914, he rode the crest of his popularity. Clarence Clenenden explains, "To innumerable Mexicans during the agonizing years of the Mexican Revolution, Francisco Villa was almost a Messiah; he was the devoted leader who would guide the forgotten man of Mexico--the peon--to comfort and plenty."[4] Seven months after leaving El Paso on stolen horses, Villa and his men had become such a formidable military force that the Federal Mexican Army had evacuated the northern province of Chihuahua and he won a strategic victory almost by default. Pancho Villa, an ignorant, illiterate peasant who spoke *pelado*, the crude Spanish dialect of the poor, had become the strong man in command of northern Mexico.

After taking Juarez, Villa knew he would have to defend it against the Mexican federal army, or *Federales*. Texans in El Paso were worried about rifle fire crossing the Rio Grande River. Villa assured Mayor Kelley of El Paso that he would fight the *Federales* far enough away so that no bullets would

note
x Clendenen

reach the United States. Francisco Villa kept his word, but his attitude towards Americans soon changed.

Larry Harris writes about Villa's formative years, but his book focuses on the Columbus raid. This event in American history seems inconsequential to us now, yet in March of 1916, the eighteen dead Americans killed by a ragtag band of Mexican revolutionaries created a political crisis. The United States responded to the killings as if they were an act of war. Villa and his mounted troops attacked the town of Columbus, New Mexico, in a two-and-one-half hour pre-dawn raid on March 6, 1916. By March 15, Brigadier General John "Black Jack" Pershing had 4,800 U.S. troops from Fort Bliss, Texas, on the march in pursuit of Villa.

Causes of the raid remain obscure. Scholars have argued that President Wilson had infuriated Villa by supporting the Mexican leader Carranza who had become Villa's archenemy. Wilson had allowed Mexican federal troops to use American railroads to gain faster access to defend Agua Prieta on the Mexican border near Douglas, Arizona, against Villa's attack. Federal troops soundly defeated the *Villistas* and Francisco was furious at President Wilson. On January 17, 1916, *Villistas* stopped a train at Santa Isabel, Mexico, and killed seventeen United States mining engineers. Although Villa was far away at the time and could not have communicated with his supporters, they would have known of his hardened attitude towards Americans.

Villa may have attacked Columbus in retribution against the United States, though as Frederich Katz states in his article in the *American Historical Review,* Villa believed a plot existed between Carranza and the United States to make Mexico an economically dependent protectorate. Katz even claims collusion among the Standard Oil Company, other business interests and the Department of State to finance a new Mexican leader.[5]

Perhaps Villa attacked Columbus to turn the tables on Carranza, because Villa guessed that U.S. troops would invade Mexico and create a diplomatic and military imbroglio for his enemy Carranza. If those were Villa's intentions, his ruse worked. The United States and Mexico almost came to war and

Mexicans perceived Americans as aggressors and Villa as a national hero. Other stories suggest that Villa had money in the bank in Columbus which he needed to withdraw and that he attempted to retrieve guns and ammunition from the Columbus hardware merchant San Ravel, who had failed to deliver goods Villa had ordered.

Author William McGaw speculates that Associated Press writer George L. Seese paid Villa $80,000 in cash to conduct the raid as an excuse to mobilize American forces to invade Mexico.[6] If the raid was a deliberate attempt to test America's military responsiveness, it was an unqualified success. Pershing had 4,800 U.S. troops in Mexico within six days and would soon have 10,000 American soldiers. Mobilization continued with 110,957 officers and enlisted men at the border along with 40,139 National Guardsmen.[7]

The most intriguing theory behind the Columbus raid focuses on German involvement in Mexico. The authors of *La Frontera*, a recent book on the Mexican-American border or frontier, claim the Germans had hoped to create a diversion along the border and had planted Dr. Lyman Rauschbaum on Villa's staff as a secretary and bookkeeper. Rauschbaum could have convinced Villa that the State Bank of Columbus had cheated him of $10,000.[8] There is no doubt that Villa's men used seven millimeter German Mausers and wore bandeliers carrying as many as 300 rounds.

German provocateurs may have urged Villa to attack the United States and start a border war, but the complete Mexican-German connection occurred after the Columbus raid when the Mexican government sent a memo to Germany proposing economic and military cooperation to rid Mexico of Pershing's troops. Germany replied with a telegram to Mexico in 1917 written by Foreign Secretary Arthur Zimmerman suggesting a German-Mexican alliance. If Germany won the war, Mexico was to received Arizona, New Mexico and Texas-- territory seized from Mexico in 1848 by the United States. Exposure of the telegram helped turn U.S. sentiment against Germany and contributed to the entry of the United States in World War I.[9]

If the Germans thought that American involvement in a border conflict would prohibit the United States from entering a European war, they were mistaken. In fact, the United States Army learned invaluable lessons in their fruitless pursuit of Villa across the Mexican states of Chihuahua and Sonora. The army also learned lessons during the raid itself. As *Villistas* swooped into Columbus to attack the town, American soldiers fired their Benet-Mercier machine guns which repeatedly jammed. After the raid, Columbus became the first U.S. Army Air base in history. Primitive Curtis-Jennie biplanes flew off from Columbus only to crash in the desert.

By the end of April, 1916, four planes had been lost. The Report of Operations for the First Aero Squadron explains that, "All flying officers were continuously called upon to take extraordinary risks in every reconnaissance flight made while on duty in Mexico." Major Foulois noted, "All officers thoroughly appreciated the fact that the failure of their aeroplane motors, while flying through mountainous canyons and over rugged mountains, would invariably result in death."[10] No officers died, but there were several close calls, and a few comical incidents.

Ordered to fly at night to Casas Grandes, Mexico, from Columbus, New Mexico, Lt. Edgar S. Gorrell explains:

> Only Lieutenant Dodd had ever flown at night. The rest of us had never been off the ground after dusk . . . We had no maps, only blueprints which someone thought was a representation of the country south of the border. We had no reliable compasses, and such as they were, each airplane was equipped with a different type. There were no lights on the planes and when the sun went down we could not see any of the instruments.[11]

Because of darkness and low fuel Gorrell landed in the middle of a cow pasture. Fearful for his life and afraid of unfriendly Mexicans, he relates:

I took out my pistol, canteen of water, emergency rations and blueprint map from the cockpit . . . I dropped to my stomach and started to crawl. [Followed by a herd of cattle and horses] I crawled forward [and] the herd came after me; when I stopped crawling, the herd stopped. When I started crawling again, the cattle and the horses would start forward, and eventually they came so close their lowered heads and horns touched my heels . . . I jumped up and started running as hard as I could toward [a] stream of water. The herd started running, too.[12]

Obviously horses and cattle on Mexican ranches were not accustomed to airplanes landing at night and pilots crawling on their bellies, but then the use of airplanes and other mechanized equipment was new to the Army. In 1916, the regular U.S. Army numbered less that 100,000 men and included only 54 trucks and thirteen planes, eight of which were headquartered in Columbus. Trucks were utilized on Pershing's "Punitive Expedition," though the chain-driven vehicles manufactured by White and Quad were poorly designed with bone-wrenching hard rubber wheels, and gas tanks dangerously located directly behind the drivers' seats. Fuel supply lines were maintained by pack animals. Perhaps Villa should be credited for bringing the U.S. military into the twentieth century. He certainly toughened up new recruits.

Pershing's men traveled south in March, and by mid-summer were faced with intense desert heat, freezing cold nights, lack of water, poor food supplies, an inhospitable civilian population, and utter frustration as they sought to punish Villa, only to have him elude their grasp. However, the American army needed the drill practice. War in Europe had begun two years earlier in 1914, and the U.S. was to enter World War I in 1917. The ten months Pershing spent chasing Villa across northern Mexico provided invaluable training for his enlisted men and officers, including a young lieutenant named George Patton.

In addition to the opportunity for military exercises, rumors persisted that the United States had invaded Mexico to acquire its northern provinces. At least one local newspaperman relished the potential of annexing portions of Mexico. Earl Ely of the *Deming Graphic*, a small newspaper in Deming, New Mexico, just north of Columbus, wrote on June 2, 1916.

> There is only one man who has the power to initiate the conquest of Mexico. That man is President Wilson. No one man has the power to stay it long. The natural law controlling the expansion of races is operating here. As yet the pressure is light and Mexico, under good government, might have stayed the Anglo-Saxon for another generation. American capital in large quantities has already been invested in Mexico . . . but when the American settlers pour into the rich valleys in numbers, the flag will soon follow . . . Mexico is a "white man's" land and made to be occupied by an industrious, virtuous, and war-like race.[13]

Despite Ely's jingoism, the last thing President Wilson wanted was permanent occupation in the northern half of Mexico. On February 9, 1917, Wilson ordered Pershing to withdraw after serious clashes with federal Mexican troops at Parral had stopped American soldiers from going further south. The United States Army had failed to find a border bandit. Pancho Villa had eluded thousands of American troops and had even foiled a recently-discovered assassination plot.

Historians Charles H. Harris and Louis R. Sadler have uncovered evidence that the U.S. Army hired Japanese nationalists as spies to move among the *Villistas* in the disguise of peddlers to give Villa a slow-acting poison. An FBI report for September 13, 1916, outlines the plan though Pershing and others on his staff so carefully concealed the records that it took seventy-two years to unravel the plot. Harris and Sadler are convinced that "as a direct response to the Mexican Revolution of 1910" including the Villa raid on Columbus, "there came into being for the first time an American Intelligence Community."[14]

Though Pershing tried to poison him, Villa survived to become a folk hero who finally disbanded his men and retired to a 25,000 acre estate called Canutillo in the northern part of Durango, his native state. At last he was home and the revolutionary laid down his arms--except for the pistol he always carried--and became interested in agriculture, education, and repairing and improving the hacienda he had acquired for himself and his loyal *Villistas*. Villa had a school built for children who lived on the hacienda and he regularly visited classes. Francisco arranged for a collective marriage ceremony for his men who had taken common law wives from among the *soldaderas* who had followed the campaigns.

Occasionally he granted interviews, and to the American journalist Frazier Hunt, Villa said, "I fought . . . so that poor men could live like human beings, have their own land, send their children to school and have human freedom. But it wasn't much use. Most of them were too ignorant to understand the [revolutionary] ideas." Villa added, "Nothing much can be done at all until the common people are educated."[15]

If Villa brought order and prosperity to the hacienda he acquired, he also brought prosperity to the town he attacked. The little border town of Columbus, New Mexico, which Villa raided in 1916, was only a nine-year-old railroad town with a smattering of houses and a few commercial buildings. The town had been struggling along on a spur railroad line with only a few farmers and ranchers to support the local economy. Thanks to Villa's raid the town immediately swelled from 300 to 10,000 people in the only spurt of growth and true prosperity the town has even known. Most of the newcomers were soldiers sent to guard the United States border. Not only did Pancho Villa cause the town of Columbus to grow but he also greatly increased the number of available U.S. troops.

Because of Villa the United States Congress passed the National Defense Act on June 1, 1916, to authorize the National Guard. Three weeks later the President called the guard to active duty on the Mexican border. America had mobilized for war and though the army never captured Villa, they learned valuable lessons about equipment deficiencies, how to maintain supply lines through rugged terrain, and the problems and promise of mechanized transport.

Over one hundred Mexicans died in the Columbus raid and their bodies were piled up and burned in the desert without funeral rites. Fifteen Mexicans taken prisoner were tried by jury and hanged in Deming, New Mexico. During court testimony at least one of the revolutionaries insisted that he had no choice but to join Villa's band or watch his own house be pillaged and burned. Pancho Villa could be firm in enlisting recruits. Villa forced volunteers to ride with him and occasionally shot at their feet thus insisting that they go on. By 1916 Villa was desperate, and starvation rations included raw mule meat. Many of his men wore clothing that was little better than rags. Jesús Paez was wounded in Columbus and in a manuscript written two years after the raid, the young boy explained that Villa initiated the raid from a distance. He stated:

> After Villa got them started on their murderous task he departed far enough away to be out of danger. He always rode a fine horse, had good clothes, and had a fine saddle. His men were ragged, hungry, and dirty, and their horses and mules were half-starved and had sores under their saddles the full length . . . [16]

If Villa hung back during the fusillade of bullets from American machine guns, he nevertheless managed to keep his ragtag army intact. When the rebel capitulated to De La Huerta five years later, he kept fifty men for a personal escort, his elite *Dorados*, and the Mexican government permitted his officers to join the federal ranks. At the end his guerilla band included nine generals, 56 captains, 75 lieutenants, 64 sergeants, 14 corporals, and 480 soldiers.[17]

In the introduction to the book *Chasing Villa* (1934) by Col. Frank Tompkins, the author's note claims that after the raid, "Major Tompkins' small force of 29 United States Cavalrymen pursued 2,500 Mexicans under the leadership of the famous bandit."[18] Fact was becoming fiction. There were never more than five hundred *Villistas* during the Columbus raid.

The Villa legend grew and the U.S. cavalry shrank. Modern warfare would soon eliminate troopers on horseback. The Punitive Expedition is noteworthy because it was the last use of horses in a major campaign and the first use of trucks.[19] Ten months after the Punitive Expedition had begun, American soldiers marched back to Columbus, and 3,000 Mexican refugees huddled south of town. The Mexican foray was only a prelude. Soldiers who had cursed the Mexican heat and the bright and pitiless sun would die in the trenches at Verdun. Soldiers who had pursued Villa across the vast distances of Sonora and Chihuahua would long for the clear desert air of Mexico instead of the lethal mustard gas of World War I.

In death as in life, Villa achieved celebrity status. He may have ordered the execution of the compelling American writer Ambrose Bierce. A recent novel by the noted Mexican author Carlos Fuentes describes Bierce as *The Old Gringo* who came to Mexico to die.[20]

Fuentes also describes Villa as "a man of the north, tall and robust, his torso longer than his short Indian legs, but with long arms and powerful hands" whose clothing had "a patina of gunpowder, thorn, and rock, pine trails and endless, blinding plains." Fuentes explains that Villa wore "a large gold-embroidered sombrero, a sombrero stained with dust and blood, not a luxury but an instrument of power and a symbol of struggle, like his wide, calloused hands and his bronze stirrups buffed by the mountain winds."[21]

The same year that Larry Harris published this book on Villa in 1949, the Texas folklorist J. Frank Dobie published *Tongues of the Monte* and added to the Villa legend by describing a forced march across the treacherous Mexican desert, the Bolson de Mapimí. According to Dobie, Pancho Villa "set out from the ancient mining town of Mapimi with 1,200 men; when four days later he reached Los Jacales to the west, he had only 900 men and many less than that number of horses." Dobie states, "During the four days neither man nor beast had come to water." J. Frank Dobie also tells of a lull during a ballad about Pancho Villa in which Dobie's Mexican host described Villa's ability to transform himself in time of danger into an ant that crawled into the belly of a dead horse "there to await the going away of the enemy. Then he emerged and was his proper self again."[22]

Legend also records Villa's smoldering anger. Villa feuded violently with Giuseppli Garibaldi, grandson of the Italian liberator, and Pancho even crossed into El Paso to kill him, but he was disarmed by friends. Certainly he caused consternation for Jolly Garner, a U.S. Customs Agent who fled the Commercial Hotel which Villa's men set ablaze in Columbus. Garner's brother, John Nance Garner, became vice-president under Franklin Delano Roosevelt. Other prominent men whose lives intersected with Villa's included Mexican and American government officials, wealthy citizens, newspaper reporters, and industrial magnates like J.P. Morgan, who may have prevented Villa's success by buying the bullets Villa had ordered. After President Wilson denied arms shipments to Villa, Morgan and others bought out the cartridge contract the revolutionary had ordered. The bullets went to France rather than to Mexico.

Despite Villa's heroic status, he had his enemies. After a night of lovemaking in Parral, Chihuahua, Villa and seven of his men in a large Dodge touring car began the forty-seven mile drive home. At 7:20 a.m. they rounded a corner down the Calle Juarez and were ambushed. Only one man survived. Pancho Villa himself received thirteen bullet wounds, but he killed one of his attackers with a pistol shot. His body was laid in state in his own Hotel Hidalgo, and he was buried in Parral on July 21, 1923. The life of the bandit revolutionary had come to an end.

Forty-three years after his assassination, by an act of the Mexican Congress, Francisco Villa became an official hero of the Revolution. William Weber Johnson in his epic study *Heroic Mexico* (1968), discusses Madero, Carranza, Obregon, Zapata and Villa. Johnson explains "All of them were heroes, all were martyrs by assassination, and almost all were mutually antagonistic and incompatible. Their only common ground was service to the Revolution . . ."[23] Other authors have commented on Villa's visual presence and his dynamic poses which proclaimed him a revolutionary for the cameras and newsmen. Carlos Monsivais writes, "Villa and Zapata . . . are ahead of their time: if they are the manifest symbols of the Revolution it is because they focus and develop the visual elements." Monsivais explains, "Only a revolution could anticipate the motion picture's use of the close-up," which is a cinematic technique that Villa utilized to the hilt.[24]

Photographs of Villa endure and books about him continue to be written. Larry Harris's text lapses into occasional errors and inaccuracies, particularly with body counts in the Columbus raid. There are also disputes over how many bodyguards were on duty the day Villa was killed, but overall Harris's text contains the urgency of truth, the flavor of folklore, and the sparkle of legend. Represented here, it tells the story of a man who rose against the bitter oppression of the Mexican caste system to become a leader who would hear his name and the chant "Viva Villa" echo off crumbling adobe walls in dozens of poor villages where there had been no hope and no future. Villa promised both. A true man of the people, his name lives on.

Endnotes

[1] For folk songs listen to the contemporary ballad "Pancho & Lefty" recorded by Willie Nelson. For Villa's stature as a bandit see John Reed, *Insurgent Mexico*. 1914. (New York: Greenwood Press, 1969): 117.

[2] Reed, p. 118. Reed was an avowed socialist and so was Jack London, but London's coverage of the Revolution for *Collier's Magazine* only helped convince the American public that President Wilson's protectionist stance was correct. See Rodolfo G. Serrano, "Revolution: Jack London and the Mexican 'Peon'." Unpublished paper presented at the 1988 Popular Culture Association, Annual Conference, St. Louis, Missouri.

[3] Reed, p. 121. Author John Reed explains on page 121 that Villa had stolen the horses which he took when he left El Paso in April of 1913. Reed adds a postscript: "Six months later, when Villa came triumphantly into Juarez at the head of an army of four thousand men,

the first public act he committed was to send a man with double the price of the horses to the owner of the livery stable."

4 Clarence C. Clenenden, *The United States and Pancho Villa* (Ithaca, New York: Cornell University Press, 1961):11.

5 Frederich Katz, "Pancho Villa and the Attack on Columbus, New Mexico," *American Historical Review* (83.1, 1978): 121.

6 William McGaw. See "Secrets Will Out" in *Southwest Saga* (Phoenix: Golden West Publishers, 1988): 134-140.

7 McGaw, *Southwest Saga*, p. 139.

8 Alan Weisman and Jay Dusard, *La Frontera: The United States Border with Mexico* (New York: Harcourt, Brace, Jovanovich, 1984): 104.

9 For a thorough examination of this topic by a Pulitzer price winning historian see Barbara Tuchman, *The Zimmerman Telegram* (New York: The MacMillan Co., 1958). In the 1980s revisionist historians are paying a great deal of attention to the impact that Mexico had on President Wilson's foreign policies. Most new documentary films on World War I now mention the Punitive Expedition and Wilson sending Pershing to find Villa. Other cinematic accounts of the Mexican Revolution include "A Fistful of Dynamite" starring James Coburn as an Irish revolutionary who blew up Federal trains, and the awful portrayal of Villa by Telly Savalas in "Pancho Villa." The film is definitely B grade, though "A Fistful of Dynamite" has redeeming qualities. Another period film is "Villa Rides" with Yul Brynner, Charles Bronson and Robert Mitchum as a U.S. Army pilot.

10 A good recent review of the First Aero Squadron is inGwendolyn Fayne, "The 1916 Mexican Punitive Expedition: The Action-packed Adventure of the First Aero Squadron in Mexico," unpublished manuscript. Presented at the Rocky Mountain American Studies Association meeting in Albuquerque, NM, March 1987. Fayne teaches at the United States Air Force Academy which holds the records of the First Aero Squadron. For Foulois statement see p. 10.

[11] Fayne, "First Aero Squadron," p. 4.

[12] Fayne, p. 5.

[13] Earl Ely quoted in Bill Rakocy, *Villa Raids Columbus, New Mexico, March 9, 1916*, (El Paso, TX: Bravo Press, 1981): 100.

[14] Charles H. Harris and Louis R. Sadler, *The Border and the Revolution*, (Las Cruces: New Mexico State University, 1988): 23. Information on Japanese nationalist spies is from the chapter "Termination with Extreme Prejudice: The United States Versus Pancho Villa."

[15] William Weber Johnson, *Heroic Mexico* (New York: Harcourt, Brace, Jovanovich, 1968): 364.

[16] Jesús Paez, "The Villa Raid and Jesús Paez," unpublished manuscript dated 1918 in the collections of the Deming-Luna Mimbres Museum, Deming, New Mexico, page 5. For a description of the Columbus Raid recorded by the New Mexico Federal Writers Project in the 1930s, see Marta Weigle and Peter White, *The Lore of New Mexico* (Albuquerque: University of New Mexico Press, 1988): 290-292.

[17] Johnson, *Heroic Mexico*, p. 362.

[18] Frank Tompkins, *Chasing Villa* (Harrisburg, PA: Military Service Publishing Co., 1934): page VII.

[19] To understand the U.S. Army's use of the cavalry and the training that "Black Jack" Pershing received see Donald Smythe, "John J. Pershing: Frontier Cavalryman," *New Mexico Historical Review* (No. 3, July 1963): 220-243.

[20] McGaw in *Southwest Saga*, pp. 107-114 speculates on Villa killing Bierce. For a fictional account by a noted author who spent forty years researcing folk tales about Ambrose Bierce, see Carlos Fuentes, *The Old Gringo* (New York: Harper & Row, 1985). The book is soon to be a

major motion picture with Jane Fonda as the schoolteacher and Gregory Peck as Ambrose Bierce.

[21] Ibid. p. 169.

[22] J. Frank Dobie, *Tongues of the Monte* (Boston: Little, Brown & Company) pp. 251, 261.

[23] Johnson, *Heroic Mexico*, IX.

[24] Carlos Monsivais essay in Agustin Victor Casasola, *The World of Mexico: 1900-1938* (Washington, D.C.: The Fondo del Sol Visual Arts and Media Center, 1984): 50.

Selected Bibliography on Pancho Villa & the Mexican Revolution
by Andrew Gulliford, Ph.D.
Director of the Museum
Middle Tennessee State University

Aultman, Otis A. *Photographs From the Border*. El Paso: El Paso Public Library Association, 1977.

Bowman, Jon. "Pancho Villa State Park," *New Mexico Magazine* (January, 1989) pp. 17-18.

Braddy, Haldeen. *Cock of the Walk: The Legend of Pancho Villa*. Port Washington, NY: Kennikat Press, 1970.

Casasola, Agustin Victor. *The World of Mexico: 1900-1938*. Washington, D.C.: The Fondo del Sol Visual Arts and Media Center, 1984. Photo exhibit catalog funded by the Ford Motor Company Fund.

Clendenen, Clarence C. *The United States and Pancho Villa*. Ithaca, NY: Cornell University Press, 1961.

Crouch, James L. "Wings South: The First Foreign Employment of Air Power by the United States." *Aerospace Historian*. (Spring 1972): 27-31.

Dobie, J. Frank. *Tongues of the Monte*. Boston: Little, Brown & Company, 1949.

Dodd, Townsend F. "The First United States Aero Squadron: Mexican Adventures of Foulois, Carberry, Kilner and Gorrell." *U.S. Air Service*. (1919): 15-18.

El Paso Times. "Roswell man helped clean up after Villa's raid." Sunday, August 23, 1987.

Fayne, Gwendolyn. "The 1916 Mexican Punitive Expedition: The Action-packed Adventure of the First Aero Squadron in Mexico," Unpublished manuscript. Presented at the Rocky Mountain American Studies Association meeting in Albuquerque, NM, March, 1988.

Fuentes, Carlos. *The Old Gringo*. New York: Harper & Row, 1985.

Furman, Necah S. "Vida Nueva: A Reflection of Villista Diplomacy, 1914-1915." *New Mexico Historical Review:* Vol. 53, No. 2 (April 1978), pp. 171-192.

Guzman, Martin Luis. *Memoirs of Pancho Villa*. Austin, TX: University of Texas Press, 1965.

Harris, Charles H. and Louis R. Sadler. "Pancho Villa and the Columbus Raid." *New Mexico Historical Review*. Vol. L. No. 4 (Oct. 1975), pp. 335-346.

_____. *The Border and the Revolution*. Las Cruces: New Mexico State University, 1988.

Johnson, William Weber. *Heroic Mexico*. New York: Harcourt, Brace, Jovanovich, 1968.

Katz, Frederich. "Pancho Villa and the Attack on Columbus, New Mexico." *American Historical Review* 83.1 (1978) pp. 101-130.

Machado, Manuel A. Jr., ed. *Centaur of the North: Francisco Villa, the Mexican Revolutions & Northern Mexico*. Austin, TX: Eakin Press, 1988.

Mason, Herbert Molly, Jr. *The Great Pursuit*. New York: Random House, 1970.

McGaw, William. *Southwest Saga*. Phoenix: Golden West Publishers, 1988.

Munch, Francis J. "Villa's Columbus Raid." *New Mexico Historical Review*. Vol. XLIV, No. 3. (July 1969), pp. 198-214.

Paez, Jesús. "The Villa Raid and Jesús Paez." Unpublished manuscript dated 1918 in the collections of the Deming-Luna Mimbres Museum, Deming, New Mexico.

Peterson, Jessie, and Thelma Cox Knoles, eds. *Pancho Villa: Intimate Recollections by People Who Knew Him*. New York: Hastings House Publishers, 1977.

Punitive Expedition, Headquarters of--in the field, Mexico. *"Report of Operations of "General" Francisco Villa since November 1915."* July 31, 1916. 106 pages. Air Force Academy Special Collections. Colorado Springs, Colorado.

Punitive Expedition in Camp near Colonia Dublan, Mexico. Intelligence Section. September 1, 1916. 103 pages. Air Force Academy Special Collections.

Punitive Expedition in Camp near Colonia Dublan, Mexico. June 30, 1916. War Department, April 4, 1919. Air Force Academy Special Collections.

Rakocy, Bill. *Villa Raids Columbus, New Mexico, March 9, 1916*. El Paso, TX: Bravo Press, 1981.

Reed, John. *Insurgent Mexico*. 1914. New York: Greenwood Press, 1969.

Reed, Raymond J. "The Mormons in Chihuahua, Their Relations with Villa and the Pershing Punitive Expedition, 1910-1917." M.A. Thesis. Albuquerque: University of New Mexico, 1938.

Report of the Operations of the First Aero Squadron, Signal Corps, With Punitive Expedition, U.S.A., for Period March 15 to August 15, 1916. Columbus, New Mexico, 1916. U.S. Air Force Academy Special Collections.

Schuster, Ernest Otto. *Pancho Villa's Shadow.* New York: Exposition Press, 1947.

Serrano, Rodolfo G. "Revolution: Jack London and the Mexican 'Peon'." Unpublished paper presented at the 1988 Annual Meeting of the Popular Culture Association, St. Louis, Missouri.

Tompkins, Frank, Col. *Chasing Villa.* Harrisburg, PA: Military Service Publishing Co., 1934.

Torres, Elias L. *Twenty Episodes in the Life of Pancho Villa.* Austin, TX: Encino Press, 1973.

Tuchman, Barbara. *The Zimmerman Telegram.* New York: MacMillan, Co., 1958.

Weigle, Marta and Peter White. *The Lore of New Mexico.* Albuquerque: University of New Mexico Press, 1988.

Weisman, Alan and Jay Dusard. *La Frontera: The United States Border with Mexico.* New York: Harcourt, Brace, Jovanovich, 1984.

"What U.S. Troops May Encounter in Pursuing Villa." *New York Tribune.* 19 March 1916.

Williams, Vernon L. "Lieutenant George S. Patton, Jr. and the American Army: On the Texas Frontier in Mexico, 1915-1916," *Military History of Texas and the Southwest,* Vol. 17, no. 1 (1982).

Generals Villa and Orozco at the Elite Confectionery, El Paso,
1911. Courtesy El Paso Public Library.

Soldados of the Revolution. Courtesy El Paso Public Library.

A company of *Rurales* (federal rural militia) loading horses.

U.S. Army motorpool in Mexico, 1916. Courtesy El Paso Public Library.

Felipe Angeles, Villa's master of artillery, 1914.

Identifying dead *Federales* and collecting them for burial, 1915.

Public executions were common during the Revolution.

U.S. Cavalry and dead Mexican soldier, 1916.

After the Raid. Courtesy El Paso Public Library.

Soldadera. Courtesy El Paso Public Library.

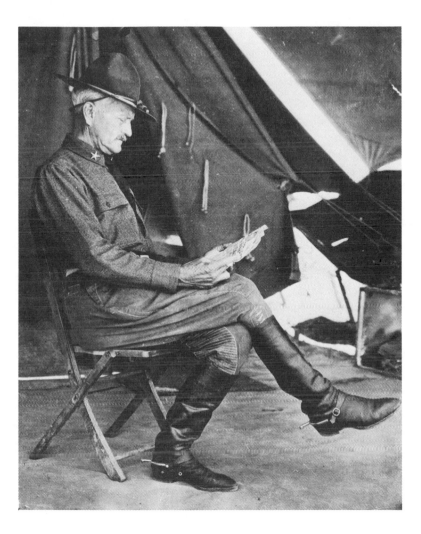

General John J. Pershing in Mexico, 1916.

Larry A. Harris (1903 - 1966), a native of Indiana, lived most of his life in El Paso. A graduate of Wabash College and lifetime journalist, he wrote over 600 western short stories and novels before finishing his career as an executive for KROD-TV, El Paso.

PANCHO VILLA

AND

THE COLUMBUS RAID

By

LARRY A. HARRIS

Author of "The Maverick Legion",
"Old Texas Days", "The Fighting Texicans", etc.

•

SUPERIOR PRINTING, INC.
EL PASO, TEXAS

•

Copyright, 1949, Larry A. Harris

Photo of Villa in dress uniform, autographed by Pancho and presented by him personally to the late Dr. Herbert E. Stevenson of El Paso as a token of his admiration for the doctor.

Pancho Villa and one of his wives, Austreberta Renteria Vda. de Villa.

Top: After the capture of Juarez, Villa and his men head south to win all of Chihuahua.
Below: A rare photo of Pancho with his brother Hipolito, who acted as cashier and purchasing agent for Villa.

Top: A Villista sniper harassing enemy troops prior to the attack on Chihuahua City.

Below: Villa troopers loading on a train in the Juarez yards for the triumphant ride to Mexico City.

Top: Villa's men lolling along a tree-lined ditch bank, waiting for word to attack the outskirts of Chihuahua.
Below Bodies of dead Federalista soldiers killed by artillery fire in the battle of Torreon.

Top: Villa's soldados departing from Torreon after sacking the town.

Below: An artillery piece firing on Chihuahua City. Soldier in big hat, third from right, is Tracy Richardson, the American soldier of fortune.

Top: American ranchers and civilians who organized after the Columbus raid to help U. S. troops protect the border.

Below: American soldiers of the 13th Cavalry hold a confab with Mexican civilians along the fence line where Villa and his men crossed into the U. S.

Top: American soldiers crossed into Mexico in March, 1916.
Below: In Columbus, New Mexico, today are ruins, boarded-up buildings and brush-littered streets—reminders of the Villa raid.

Contents

Acknowledgements

The author wishes to thank the following people, who, had they not given of their time, patience and information, this book never could have been written.

JESS FULLER, who, the night of the Columbus raid, got in some good shots, but was entranced by the Villista bugler.

FLOYD BLAIR, blind now, but whose memories have never dimmed.

G. C. TROWBRIDGE, a bank president now, who was a sergeant in Company I, New Mexico National Guard, stationed at Columbus.

'SUS CARREON, a merchant in Columbus, who as a youth the night of the raid, did his damdest to save a herd of mules.

PABLO GOMEZ, who, though executed by the Federalistas, refused to die.

MANUEL GONZALES, a Villa confidante and soldier.

JOSE JUARRIETA, Villa's aide-de-camp and true Mexican patriot, who went through six years of revolution and came out with the facts.

PERRO NEGRO, Black Dog, the nameless viejo who, as caretaker of the Juarez cemetery, witnessed the execution of seventy-five Villa traitors one morning, and who managed to keep one of the bodies.

WILLIAM D. GREET, El Pasoan, whose memory will always be revered by those who knew him. He told me much, but not enough.

LOUISA VILLA, Pancho's favorite niece, who as a beautiful young lady, remembered her uncle's laughter when he played piggyback with her.

FERNANDO PALACIO3, who almost bought a battleship.

THE SOLDIERS OF FORTUNE, the nameless Mexican soldados, and numerous others who, adherents of the old adage that a sleeping dog should remained undisturbed, have requested that their names be omitted.

THE EL PASO TIMES, Editor Bill Hooten; Publisher Dorrance D. Roderick, and many of the staff who gave me complete access to their files.

BEN TURNER, a prominent business man in El Paso, and one-time Colonel with Villa, a cherished friend of mine of long standing, whose adventures with Villa must someday be compiled into a book.

BRUCE STEELE, former soldier of fortune with Villa, veteran of two South American revolutions, whom Villa called "Santiago", who was entrusted with the diamond loot, whose story of the Villa Revolution is both tragic and hilariously funny.

RALPH WILSON, photographer and Villa historian, whose fine pictures of present-day Columbus, New Mexico, appear in this book, along with the author's collection.

Prologue

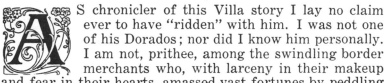

S chronicler of this Villa story I lay no claim ever to have "ridden" with him. I was not one of his Dorados; nor did I know him personally. I am not, prithee, among the swindling border merchants who, with larceny in their makeup and fear in their hearts, amassed vast fortunes by peddling the naive Villa worthless ammunition, antiquated rifles and nondescript uniforms. They ran the gamut of deceit and thievery, these cringing tycoons of hockshop ancestry, only to, in later years, become the most stalwart advocates of the Good Neighbor policy, fair trade practices and brotherly love. When word came from Parral in 1923 that Pancho Villa, the rebel, was dead they heaved Pontius Pilate sighs of relief.

If all the men who claim to have ridden with Villa had actually done so, Pancho's rebel battalions would have made Mexico resemble a human ant hill. The Texas border nurtures lurid tales; around roundup campfires and in cantinas prodigious stories are told of the Villa days: of bloody battles and forays, of robust encounters and of executions. There is humor in some of the stories; there are hilarious incidents told, and recounts of deep tragedies. And, granting the raconteurs a poetic license, you listen, trying to determine the thin line between fact and fancy. Often it is hard. Memory is both subtle and vicious. It is easy for an oldtimer to drift with his dreams. He is not offensive with his tall tales. You listen to him, enthralled by his dramatic discourse, and you justifiably excuse him if his grasshopper monograph does not exactly coincide with historical facts.

If this book is a patchwork quilt, remember that Villa's life was of the same pattern. For twenty-two years I have collected Villa legend and lore. At times it seemed hopeless, dove-tailing the various incidents of his life, seeking verification of certain conflicting incidents. Over the years I have visited strange places and met stranger people. And now in this actual writing I promise one thing: to stick to facts as rigidly as humanly possible — facts derived from those persons who lived with Pancho Villa and knew him; who actually rode with him, watched him laugh and watched him kill. And who knew him for what he truly was.

I have tried to exclude prejudice in this writing, or fanciful flights into the dramatic. I have known intimately Americans and Mexicans who were members of Villa's famed Dorados, and from all walks of life they came: soldiers of fortune, gamblers, thieves with prices on their heads, patriots and preachers, men with ugly memories, and just men. At nights, over *copitas*, in side street cantinas, along the border and in Mexico, I have listend to them and watched their eyes glow in the lamplight as they re-lived those fabulous days of Pancho Villa.

It was in 1927 — while precariously on the payroll of the *El Paso Times* — that I first met Otis Aultman. He operated a photograph shop adjoining the newspaper, probably the most unorthodox camera shop Texas ever has known. Otis was wiry, short and wizened; he was in constant need of a haircut; he was wrinkled, ageless and a profound bottle man. Like an animated gargoyle he pranced through life, alternately grinning and snarling, hating hypocrisy and loving the humble. His contempt for people was a delightful thing; and for convention he cared not a whit.

Otis, a voracious eater, was a steady patron at Gus the Greek's restaurant. One night while sitting with him at the crowded counter I noticed him scrutinizing another man farther down the row of diners. Otis squirmed until he had gulped his last bite. Then he walked to where the stranger was sitting and stuck out his hand. The man, slightly nonplussed, accepted the handshake.

"Mister," Otis said, "I don't know your name, but I want to shake your hand. Until now I've been known as the ugliest man in El Paso, and I've accepted that dubious honor gracefully. However, I'm conferring my title upon you from now on. Any fair minded judge will back me up. You are, unquestionably, the ugliest man in El Paso."

The man thus addressed was a prominent El Paso attorney, an oldtimer. Why he and Otis had never met before was a peculiar quirk of fate. He was definitely no Adonis; but his lack of physical beauty was offset by a Friar Tuck sense of humor. He accepted his extra-curricular degree in good grace. From that night on he and Otis were the closest of friends.

Otis had been Villa's official photographer. He went through the entire revolutionary campaign in Mexico. Steeped in the philosophy of fatalism, profane and unpredictable, he won Villa's heart because he was a firebrand and an indigenous rebel. Legend has it that he was the only man to curse Villa and live. Perhaps Villa admired the bantam rooster display of gall on the part of the little gringo.

Villa always hated luxury. However, he was enthralled when Otis presented him with a toilet seat for his private railway coach. Otis had the porcelain stool piped for water. The more squeamish of Villa's aides, shaken by the audacity of Otis' gift, predicted all sorts of horrendous tidings.

Instead of rage, Villa's round face broke into a grin when he saw the bathroom gadget. He flushed it not once but repeatedly. His joy was a sight to behold. He lowered and lifted the white enameled lid.

"Thank you, Little Rooster," he told Otis.

"*Por nada,*" said Otis.

"Tomorrow, or the next day, Little Rooster, you can show me how you *Americanos* bathe in things so small."

While with Villa, Otis came to know Floyd Gibbons, who was covering the revolution for the Chicago Tribune. In the same contingent were Alfred Henry Lewis of the Hearst papers, Willis of the New York Tribune, John Reed of the New York World and Gregory Mason of the Outlook. When the revolutionary hi-jinks in Mexico had quieted, these robust jornalists were qualified as war correspondents for the big uproar in Europe.

In the summer of 1928, just prior to the Escobar Revolution in Mexico, I spent many leisure hours in the rear of Otis' photograph shop, while he puttered in and out of the dark room with dripping negatives. Atop this dark room, reached by a rickety ladder, was his cot and littered articles of clothing — a boudoir of many odors and empty whiskey bottles. It was from the top of this slumber-perch that Otis, woozy and weary with a world at which he had thumbed his nose, fell one night and died of a broken neck.

I knew Otis well, and was his friend, who saw in him the great attributes of integrity and native intelligence. By connoiseurs who knew photography he was acclaimed a genius — after his death. He had all the humility and modesty of a berserk Irishman at the keyboard of a caliope on St. Patrick's Day, this confirmed bachelor of acidulous tongue. He had the hands of a blacksmith and the soul of a poet. Yet beneath a tough crust he was sensitive and generous and forever kind.

Otis' constant companion was a lop-eared, long-limbed dog of uncertain ancestry. This spotted mongrel, asleep or awake, seemed constantly aware of Otis' presence; they were inseparable. Elmer was the animal's name, but never did I hear Otis address him by his surname alone. It was always with deepest affection that he would say, "Come here Elmer-You-Old-Son-Of-A-Bitch."

This is a story of Pancho Villa, and the lack of space alone is a mandate for brevity. However, no biography of Pancho would be complete without digressing briefly for an insight into the colorful lives of just a few of the men who helped guide Villa's destiny; who fought his battles, shared his glory and humiliation, hungered and hell raised, looted and loved — and lived to tell it.

I remember the hot El Paso sun that streamed through the rear door of Otis Aultman's place. There were always buzzing flies, it seemed, and the gentle whimper of Elmer-You-Old-Son-Of-A-Bitch as Otis shared his sugared whiskey. I look back, deep in memories, recalling these vital men who made history with Villa, and feel grateful that they of that era should have shared their friendship with me, a nosey young man at the time, enamored of life.

The Rio Grande and Old Mexico were only six blocks to the south of the *Times* building. Juarez was sinisterly quiet in 1928; but it was a whispery hush which presages a storm. Otis and I stood in the old Crystal Palace Bar, feeling the tension that strums at one's nerves. Two American border patrolmen had been killed in less than a year. Guns and ammunition were crossing the river into Mexico.

"How soon will it be, Otis?" I asked.

Otis grinned, but his eyes mirrored the sight of fresh blood in the sun-baked dust. "Next March 1," he said. "You'll see a good one. Not as good, of course, as in 1911 when Bruce Steele, Garibaldi and Tracy Richardson — all three drunk at the time — saved the battle by throwing homemade hand-grenades over the walls of the Juarez garrison and capturing it singlehanded. As a reward Villa gave them ten thousand *pesos*, a horse apiece and three of his favorite women. Nonetheless, this next one will be all you'll want. Where's that beer you were going to order, Horace Greeley?"

Otis missed the starting date of the Escobar Revolution by two days.

In that rear room, by way of the alley door, I saw strange men come and go: tan-faced men with restless eyes. They were of an era now long dead. They had helped make history — in the banana republics of South America, with Villa in Torreon and Chihuahua, with the French Foreign Legion in African outposts. They were quiet-

spoken rebels with an allergy for society. They scorned
death and laughed at life.

They were a strange fraternity, those men. Without
exception they were soft spoken and self-effacing. They
sensed the futility of their battle to right injustice, but
never spoke of it. Life to them was an erratic play,
prompted by death; and when the curtain call came, other
performers could take the bows, for they, restless souls,
would be off in the dark wings answering the inexplicable
siren call of new adventures.

There were Emil Holmdahl, Tracy Richardson and
Sam Dreben. Usually they were alone. After months of
unexplained absence they would enter the rear door of
Otis' place with the casual greetings of a delivery clerk.

"Things okay, Otis?"

"Okay, Tracy — or were."

They accepted me because I was a friend of Otis. They
spoke of the Villa days, and of Villa, as more academic
men speak of college wool-gatherings; they told of political
intrigue, macabre deals and queer plottings. Sometimes
they were "hot"; they never straddled a political fence.
They were either for or against.

From them I learned many things about Villa. Never
did I pose before them as a third-string Boswell, pencil
and pad in hand, and ply them with questions. And never
once did they ask me, in confidence, to refrain from bandy-
ing their remarks on newsprint. That was understood. In
that dingy room of cobwebs and drying negatives there
were some verbal utterances that will never be printed.

Those men are dead now, including Otis Aultman. But
much of what they did and said will long be remembered
by those who knew them.

"Tracy Richardson," Otis once said, "was with the
Princess Pats during the first World War. He got all
shot up, but recovered. Tracy was always getting himself
shot. He was always peering around corners for one more
potshot when he should have been running."

They used to call Sam Dreben "The Fighting Jew."
One day during the Mexican revolution Sam got cut off
from his outfit. When things got so hot no man in his
right mind would have stayed, Sam took off, heading for

the open country and safety. Out of firing range Sam still was breaking all records for the hundred yard dash when he came upon Tracy Richardson.

Tracy was sprawled out beneath a tree with blood spurting from his chest where he had been shot.

"What can I do for you, Tracy?" Dreben panted.

"Just light a cigarette and poke it in my mouth, Sam," Tracy said.

"I've got cigarettes but no matches," said Dreben.

"Then go back to town and get some matches."

Dreben returned to town where the battle still was raging. An hour later he returned to where Richardson lay — with an enemy doctor as hostage, matches and two quarts of tequila.

Sam Dreben, a Russian Jew, was bullet-headed and squat-built. He had been a soldier of fortune all over the world, in wars big and little. One thing about him: he had the gall of an army mule and was one of the bravest men I ever knew.

One night in 1932 a friend phoned me at home. I knew him as a sane man, not given to hysteria or alcoholic hallucinations.

"Richardson just crossed the border two jumps ahead of the rurales, and not wounded — for some strange reason. Word is that he opened Villa's grave and cut of his head. They say the craniometrists at the University of Chicago offered him ten thousand dollars for the old boy's head . . . ."

I hurried down to the old Sheldon Hotel, knowing that Richardson had, in the past, used the hostelry's back rooms as a sanctuary. He wasn't there. I went from there down to Aultman's photo shop and found it dark. For a week I haunted the place, but Otis was gone. Wild rumors flew around El Paso like crows in a dust storm; the police knew nothing; the Mexican customs shrugged.

A drunken newspaperman, who when sober was more than a little mad, told me: "Sure he's got Villa's head. Got it buried up on the side of Mt. Franklin. I'm going up there tomorrow and dig it up if somebody doesn't beat me to it. Always did want old Villa's head. Be nice to keep setting around on my dresser . . . ."

At the end of a week Otis was back, puttering around with his dripping negatives, humming off-key. He never got around to telling me where he had been, and I didn't ask too much.

"All a bunch of old wives' tales," he said. "You know damn well if Richardson had done a thing like that he'd have been wounded. And I happen to know he ain't been shot lately. Just got a letter from him postmarked Chicago."

Señora Luz Corral Villa, Pancho's first wife, lives in Ciudad Chihuahua. Her home is spacious and neatly furnished. She is a gracious lady of middle age, plump and mellow and slightly aggressive, who lives with her memories. She loves to talk of Pancho, and somehow you get the idea that he was her erring son rather than a husband. He was the only man in her life: *un gran hombre.*

Señora Villa will show you the ancient, bullet-riddled Dodge automobile in which Pancho Villa was killed that fateful day in Parral. She will guide you through her home, pointing out the family pictures on the walls. You listen to her talk, watch the expression in her eyes and you sense the unswerving love she had for the man who conquered all of Mexico. You remember that Pancho was, paradoxically, a romanticist, a lover with a bull-in-the-china-shop affinity for attractive women. Yet when his other three hot-breath marriages fizzled he, with his lagging fidelity, returned to Luz Corral. And she took him back.

"I," said *Señora* Villa recently, "have just written the true story of Pancho. I, you must remember, am his only legitimate wife. Some day I shall have it translated into English. It is the only true story of my husband."

Pancho Villa was not what the academicians call intelligent. Yet he was imbued with magnetism and charm. Men fawned upon him and he hated it. Scholars, doctors, men of brilliant minds — along with the untutored, the riff-raff and the wastrels — eagerly heeded his beck and call. He was at times the abysmal brute, a ferocious beast lusting for the blood of his enemies; a man of whimsies and hates; a man of moods and daring who, more often than history shows, was a shocking sentimentalist, kind and unobstrusively benevolent, a soft touch for children.

"He was all mans, was Pancho," Pablo Gomez once told me. "A game cock, a fighter. Wan good mans, Pancho. No capon was he, *Señor*, believe me. He had no needs for the moonlight to make love . . . ."

"He was the most uninhibited cuss I ever knew," Otis told me," — half devil and half saint, who defied the laws of man and God, and got by with it. Almost."

In my opinion he was, above all, a good salesman. Luz Corral always took him back, didn't she?

1.

Birth of A Rebel

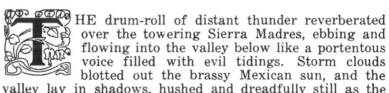

HE drum-roll of distant thunder reverberated over the towering Sierra Madres, ebbing and flowing into the valley below like a portentous voice filled with evil tidings. Storm clouds blotted out the brassy Mexican sun, and the valley lay in shadows, hushed and dreadfully still as the wind abated and the thunder quieted.

In the center of the valley the naked adobe buildings of the Hacienda Rio Grande were engulfed in gloom. Candle light suddenly shone at the windows of the main house, a sprawling, flat-roofed building with a high walled patio and garden, and more pretentious than the hovels of the *peones*. The house servants of the *hacendado*, fearful of his wrath, were preparing for the storm.

A good quarter mile away the huts and corrals of the *peones* stood in a grove of cottonwoods. The yowl of a mongrel mingled with the bray of a stray burro. The shrill cry of a buxom mother screaming at her half-naked brood came from a doorway. Pigs and chickens, wallowing in the hot red dust, roused to the sudden turmoil.

Farther across the valley a *peon* paused in his work, a hoe in hand, to glance across the tilled field toward his hut. His faded shirt was dark with sweat. As he straightened, the ache in his back was agony. In the distance the leafy limbs of the cottonwood trees were stretched skyward, as if in supplication for the sins of men.

"I wonder of Micaela, Ignacio," he mused. "With child as she is, the storm could be frightening."

The second field worker glanced up apprehensively. "I read bad omens, Augustin."

Augustin Arango smiled. "You are a man of great superstitions, Ignacio. The merciful *Dios* will be good to us, this being our first born—"

"Don Lopez," snapped Ignacio, "will have our backs lashed to bloody ribbons if he sees us loitering, *compañero*. Storm or no storm, we must hurry and finish the field."

But Augustin Arango continued to smile, even as he worked. He recalled the happiness in Micaela's eyes when he had left her for the field that morning. She had told him she wanted their first-born to be a boy; and Augustin had built a crib, fitting it into one corner of their hut near the open hearth. He'd tried to hide from Micaela the tiredness of his own body; the fact that he was not well and strong like other men.

Augustin Arango wanted a boy, not of his own image, but of Micaela's father: a strong boy, daring and brave. In whispered prayers of nights, while Micaela slept, he had asked God to provide for his child so he would never know the torture of belly hunger, the gritty, terrifying pain that came from the lash of the *mayordomo's* whip. And he prayed that the church, as represented by Father Benedito, would some day accept the union of himself and Micaela Arambula, and tender its blessing. Much of the church's doctrine, particularly the laws governing divorce and marriage, puzzled Augustin. Had not he, Augustin, when Micaela's church-wedded husband deserted her months ago, taken her in, fed her, clothed her and shown her all the tender devotion a man can know?

What mattered the pomp and ceremony of a church wedding, Augustin reasoned. Micaela was without a husband when he took her unto his own. Their love was deep and abiding; the only thing that had blighted their happiness was the refusal of the church to sanction their union. But the workers and their families at Hacienda Rio Grande, and the people in the nearby town of San Juan del Rio understood.

A crippled *viejo*, unfit for field work, came hobbling hurriedly through the gathering gloom to where Augustin and Ignacio were laboring. "Come, Augustin," the man cried excitedly. "Don Lopez says you may leave the field. Micaela is calling for you."

The storm broke in all its fury before Augustin and his companions reached their peasant abodes. Thunder boomed and lightning crashed, a kind of celestial omen presaging the turbulent life of the baby boy who was born just past midnight June 5, 1878, in the State of Durango.

Two weeks later, Augustin Arango and Micaela Arambula named their first-born Doroteo. Father Benedito, mellow with understanding, baptized little Doroteo Arango, pronounced his unqualified blessing, and the world was bright for gentle little Augustin and his mate. The other *peones* and their families at the Hacienda Rio Grande rejoiced with the parents, including Ignacio, whose foreboding of tragedy was momentarily forgotten by frequent tippling of the mescal jug.

Did Ignacio read mystic warnings in the storm that day Doroteo Arango was born? Strangely, in later years this same Doroteo Arango — then Pancho Villa — was peculiarly affected by thunder storms. He would become silent, gripped by a spell of brooding, as if his soul were attuned to the violence of the elements.

"A storm," he once said, "reminds me of a battle — man's battle to live. I mean the men I have known — the slaves of the wealthy *hacendados* and mine owners. I can close my eyes and see the rain beating down on the poor field workers. Ah, the pity that some men live in luxury while others must know belly hunger, biting cold, and the hurt of the lash. I'll change that some day!"

And to the monumental task of changing Mexico's caste system, Pancho dedicated his life, his every thought, his vast reservoir of energy. No historian ever can claim that personal gain was a factor with him. He could have retained millions in cash, along with his glory, but he scorned them both.

Villa was a complex human dynamo; a man of contradictions, a paradox. We cannot evaluate him with the yardstick of our own American philosophies or psychology. He was born in a land where violence and bloodshed were commonplace; where the yoke sores of the Spanish Conquest, under Cortez, had barely healed. For over a hundred years Mexico had known independence but the blood-red pages of history reveal an era fraught with fantastic idealism, with brutalities and romance, with revolutions and bizarre plottings.

Mexico, like other nations, has had its share of larcenous leaders who, shielding themselves behind the thin cloak of decency, schemed for their own personal gain. It has had great patriots, like Juarez, who struggled untiringly and made tremendous sacrifices to make Mexico the proud, self-governing nation it is today. Mexico has risen unashamedly from the dirt and the blood. Like other nations it has skeletons in the closet but, unlike some, it makes no virtuous effort to cover the closet door with a gaudy zarape of hypocrisy.

To understand Villa one must understand Mexico. Today there are more than thirteen million people in Mexico. They are a heterogeneous people, proud of their heritage. The blood of the Spanish dons is in them; also the blood of the Aztecs. There is no middle class. If you are born a *peon*, in bondage, the chances are you will remain there. If born of aristocratic parentage, you must retain that heritage. Some day the system may change. *Quien sabe?* Democracies work slowly.

The Mexican *peon* is fundamentally honest. He accepts life's drudgeries with fatalistic stoicism. Deeds of daring enthrall him; his plaintive songs hearken of a soul-weariness. He wants more of life, but his shrug attests volubly of the hopelessness of attaining more. Death to him is commonplace; he is scornful of it. I have seen Mexicans cry out with pain and fear when beaten in a fist fight; yet that same Mexican, when facing the firing squad, will smile contemptuously, puff on a cigarette and face death with utter scorn.

Pancho Villa was a *peon*, proudly, defiantly so. Let no historian misinterpret the zealous drive in him to change Mexico's caste system as a spiritual call. Nor did he set himself up as a divine leader. Villa was far too practical for that. He had his star, but he made that star. He worked for one end: to abolish Mexico's feudal system and eliminate the horrors of slavery. And, if in his fight to attain this end, he displayed a shocking savagery, it must be remembered that he adhered to the principle that ultimate results were worth any cost.

Villa killed his enemies; he catered to his friends. He swaggered and laughed. He never looked back, but always ahead. Time after time he hurled back defeat, shouting his defiance, when lesser men would have gone down to crushing ignominy. Given to violent fits of rage, he could be the abysmal beast one moment and a weeping sentimentalist the next. Women were his weakness; his loves were many, his marriages — four. A weeping child, or a hungry one, would bring tears of compassion to his eyes.

"There were nights," said Manuel Gonzales, "when Villa and I often talked of women. He never boasted of his amorous conquests. They chased after him, not because of his physical attraction, but because he was the great Villa. He would have given them money, clothes — anything they wanted, if they had been true to him. Once he said, 'An unfaithful woman ought to be shot.' "

Villa loved a good joke. He would laugh uproariously at some Rabelaisian tale. He was as elemental as the earth itself; he robbed the rich and gave to the poor, not as a maudlin idealist, but because the poor needed help and the rich were on his despised list. He was sincere, despite what his antagonists might say; his one purpose in life was to help Mexico.

"Life is one great game," Villa once said. "If you do not kill your enemy, he will kill you. Killings are sometimes necessary to right a great wrong. I intend to keep on fighting and killing until our country is in safe hands."

He could have been president of Mexico, this "badman" with his egoistic faith in a star. Yet he turned away from the opportunity, saying, "The president of Mexico must be a good man and one of education. I do not qualify for the position. I am a soldier, and will continue to fight for what is right."

He was ribald and uncouth; he was unschooled and unpredictable. He was a fierce warrior from the Dark Ages, certainly no paragon of virtue; but deep within him was an indefineable magnetism that made him a leader. His battle cry brought men running, stirring them to a hysterical fervor: men of all creeds and races; wastrels and killers; patriots and *pelados;* men of great intelligence and breeding. He had the spark, the bravado, the quixotic charm that make men leaders. He was feared, loved, hated. He was the one and only Pancho Villa.

2.

The First Killing

IFE became intolerable for Augustin at the Hacienda Rio Grande. The field foremen under the powerful Lopez Negrete, and at the latter's insistence, wielded their back-lashings for the slightest infraction of the rules. More than that, Augustin's health failed noticeably. But despite flagging health and miserable living conditions, Augustin's family grew.

After Doroteo, two girls and two other boys were born to Augustin and Micaela: Mariana, Marquita, Hipolito and

Antonio. Except for Hipolito, little is to be heard of the other children in later life.

Doroteo was a quarrelsome youth. His fire-cracker temper got him into fights. In his early years the fierce fires of an inner rebellion revealed themselves; he was defiant and bold; he lived in abject poverty and hated it. But his flare for leadership asserted itself. The other boys trailed after him, a little awed and frightened.

Doroteo was nimble-witted. When there was an obstacle to overcome he solved the matter quickly, with the least effort, and with a native shrewdness. Said one of his boyhood playmates:

"Yes, sir, Pancho was always smart. One day several of us decided to bet who could draw the straightest line on the ground, using as the final point a tree that grew several feet away from the starting place. I was the first one, then the others followed. All of us drew our lines making a long curve. Pancho's turn came and he drew a very straight line. We asked him how he did it and this is what he told us: 'You failed because you kept your eyes on the ground. I did not. I looked at my goal and the line came out straight.' "

Doroteo was still a very small lad when Augustin died. The loss of his father was a blow to the boy. He wept bitterly. His father, he knew, would have lived longer had he not suffered from so many floggings or if he'd had one-fifth of the nourishing food that Don Lopez Negrete enjoyed.

Love and pity for his mother was a strange admixture in Doroteo; he loved his smaller brothers and sisters deeply. They had to be fed. There was to be no schooling for Doroteo. He buried his sorrows in field work, slaving long hours.

In later years Pancho Villa seldom talked of those gruelling boyhood days. It was a period of frantic yearnings and frustration; they were the fitful nightmare years of a youth whose soul cried out in anguish against the agonies of starvation and brutal punishment.

After he had won the acclaim of all Mexico, in a moment of moody retrospect, Pancho once said to a trusted colonel: "Poverty is mankind's greatest evil. A man born in slavery is one of life's greatest tragedies. The talk of peace in the world makes me laugh. There can never be peace so long as one man has his belly full and another is starving."

On rare occasions, when Pancho spoke of his boyhood,

Top: "First Chief" Venustiano Carranza (second man from left) holding a conference with his staff officers.

Below: Francisco Madero, "The Redeemer", during his brief rule as president of Mexico.

his dark eyes smoldered. He made you see the horrors of the whipping post and hear the pitiful cries of the tormented *peones.* You knew he was living again the biting cold nights of hunger, the sweltering hot days under a scorching sun when he worked in the fields, when every fibre of his being cried out from exhaustion.

At fourteen Doroteo was doing a man's work, giving the paltry pesos he earned toward the support of the family. Despite a starvation diet he developed a large frame. He was thick-chested and broad-shouldered, agile and muscular. His pantherish stride was that of a boxer, not the trudging gait of a field worker. As a boy, and in later life, his brown eyes had a magnetic, penetrating quality. He looked clear through a man, sharply and analytically — which made most people squirm. His teeth were uneven and tarnished.

Subsistence was Doroteo's greatest problem — for himself, his mother, sisters and brothers. With each passing day the fires of his restlessness grew. Storm warnings shone in his eyes. Though forced to grovel in the dirt, he hated it. He had fantastic dreams of grandeur and power. He wanted a pistol. A gun was symbolical of power to Doroteo. Some day he would have one. Some day —

He left the *hacienda* without form or formality, taking a job on a neighboring *rancho* with the promise of a livable wage. He had a deep love for horses. In a matter of days he was an adept rider. With a borrowed pistol he learned to shoot, and shoot well.

Don Lopez, of Spanish aristocracy, believed as most wealthy *hacendados:* once a slave, always a slave. You were to work and die on his land, as were your children, and your children's children. The irate Don issued orders that brought Doroteo back to the Hacienda Rio Grande in bonds. The subsequent flogging put scars on Doroteo's back that he took with him to the grave.

This punishment only served to fan the hate-flames inside Doroteo. He confided his plans to his mother. He scoffed at her frightened counsel. Some day he'd have the money to buy her and the children out of serfdom. Some day they'd have money. He'd steal — fight — kill to get it! Spaniards like Don Lopez would suffer . . . .

The brave cries of tormented youth, the heart-break sobs of a boy in agony, and no one to believe in him, only a bereaved mother whose pleadings were in vain.

Again Doroteo disappeared from the Hacienda Rio

Grande. He got a job driving a freight wagon between Guenacevi and Chihuahua City. The job paid well. His territory of operation, thought Doroteo, was beyond the domination of the all-powerful Don Lopez. But again his plans collapsed.

Don Lopez' influence reached far. On a trumped up charge of thievery he had Doroteo jailed and severely punished. For several months Doroteo languished in jail. Once, because of a slight infraction of the rules, he was severely beaten. And once more he cried out in bitter fury against the injustice of the courts, the Diaz regime and the whole lopsided social order of the country.

The fires of vengeance are unpredictable; they can smolder or erupt with explosive abruptness. Docility in a *peon* is inbred; but in Pancho Villa docility was lacking. He could, and did, bide his time while waiting for an auspicious moment to lash back at his enemies. But at no time in his cyclonic career did he display docility. He refused to be cowed. And in analyzing this rampant individualist one readily sees that his entire life was a fight, not *for* something, but *against* something.

The desire for vegeance was the driving factor inside him. It was an obsession; it was the underlying reason for the Columbus, New Mexico raid, as we shall see.

"While there in jail," he once said, "I was thrown with the lowest type of criminals. Some of those birds could read and they read to me. They told me of famous Mexican outlaws who were robbing the rich to help the poor. One of the outlaws, a great *bandido* named Parra, impressed me much. I swore then that I'd be like him some day."

After his jail sentence was served he made secret visits to the Hacienda Rio Grande to visit his mother, brothers and sisters. He found employment on various ranches, but it was his nature never to stay long in one place. He got a job as a laborer in Chihuahua City.

Most of his earnings he took to his mother. By stinting himself on food he had managed to save enough money to purchase a pistol and a horse. During those brief clandestine visits home we find him displaying a certain fatuous worldliness. His field-working friends gathered with the family group and listened in awe to Doroteo's tales of the magnificent city.

"Some day," he promised his mother, "I'll return for you and the children."

He was eighteen years of age now. There was a cherubic softness to his round face when he smiled; but there was no mirth in his dark, restless eyes.

During one visit he told his mother about a girl he had met in Chihuahua City. She was attractive, and good. Her name was Luz Corral. She had promised to be his wife. The day would come, he said, when they would have a church wedding.

He returned to Chihuahua City. Weeks later, when a letter arrived from his mother hinting of misfortune, Doroteo headed back to the ranch. Intuitively he sensed some horrible wrong. He rode up to his mother's abode boldly, scornful of Don Lopez' wrath. His mother, brothers and sisters met him with hugs and tears.

His one sister, Mariana, was not present. She was only two years younger than Doroteo, and his favorite. She was pretty and desirable. In her veins was the warm blood of Old Mexico. Her mother, like a watchful *dueña*, had discouraged the advances of the field-working swains.

Mariana, Doroteo's mother told him uneasily, had gone to the village for supplies. She would return shortly. But Doroteo read the heart-break in his mother's eyes. Later, when Mariana returned he hugged and kissed her. He *knew* then, and as he expressed it years later, "Something seemed to tear loose inside me."

The meal that night was a cheerless thing. Micaela put the younger children to bed. Mariana went to the well for water. Doroteo watched her leave. His usual swagger was gone; his temper, a raging conflagration, threatened to consume him.

"Who betrayed her, mother?" he cried out hoarsely. "Why did it have to happen? She is not to blame!"

His mother, sobbing now, said, "She will not tell me the devil's name, Doroteo."

"I'll find out mother. Let me talk to her alone when she returns."

Doroteo did talk to his sister that night. After many tears he finally wrung the truth from her. She admitted to the trifling attentions of Don Lopez' arrogant son. No, he had not mentioned marriage. That was unthinkable, the son of wealthy *hacendado* marrying a *peon* girl. The brutal assault had happened three months ago. One night.

Mariana begged her brother not to do anything drastic. She would return with him to Chihuahua, bear the child, then search for work. She pleaded, dropping to her knees, a frightened, bewildered child.

The rage in Doroteo was an ugly thing. He kissed his sister and went to bed. Next morning he left the house before other members of the family awakened. He rode up to the spacious hacienda which belonged to Don Lopez Negrete. His loaded pistol was in his coat pocket.

Much has been written about the scene that followed. One historian, in a fantastic flight of fancy, had Doroteo seeking out the town sheriff and killing him as the guilty man. Another recorder, adept at dialogue, portrays a high-pitched drama of tear-jerking quality and gunplay that smacks of an early movie.

The truth is, Doroteo encountered Don Lopez' abusive son. In a showdown of this sort men seldom hurl wordy accusations and wait for tiresome rebuttals. It is questionable if young Negrete was even armed; but that he was a lascivious coward cannot be denied.

Blind with rage, Doroteo whipped out his pistol and began shooting. Young Negrete wilted, his body bullet-riddled. He was dead before he hit the ground. Then Doroteo was back on his horse, riding like a demon toward the distant hills.

Doroteo Arango had killed his first man. He had taken the law of retribution into his hands. The sight of blood had not sickened him. He was one tough hombre. There would be more killings now, he knew. The soldiers of *Presidente* Diaz, or the rurales, would never catch him.

The strange thoughts that crowded into Doroteo Arango's brain that fateful day will never be known. Twelve years of banditry, killings and robbery lay ahead of him — weeks and months of bizarre travel, stranger than fiction. He was to see California, Arizona, New Mexico and Texas, a lowly tramp *peon* in gringo land. He was to rise from banditry, his name a magic word, to the glory and fame accorded national heroes.

3.

Days of Banditry

IN the wild, canyon-gashed Sierra Madres of Chihuahua, Doroteo Arango found refuge from the law. Capture now meant summary death, for Don Lopez Negrete's wrath would not tolerate the dilatory action of a *Federalista* court. He ranted with such ferocity at the laxities of the medal-bedecked state officials that many of the more uneasy *politicos* resigned their offices and found solace in a bottle.

For days Doroteo played hide and seek with the bounty-hunting rurales. Like a cub wolf he hid in dark caves when his searchers came close. To allay his hunger he ate wild berries and green mesquite beans. Finally, one day, he chanced to ride into the outlaw camp of the great *bandido,* Parra.

He was half-starved and sick, but he displayed the same audacity that was always part of him. "I want to join your band, *Señor* Parra," he said bluntly. "I have killed a man and the soldiers are after me. You can depend upon my loyalty."

Bandido Parra, a case-hardened criminal with a sentimental streak, grinned at the boldness of the desperate youth. The outlaw's men stood with leveled rifle. They were taking no chances. Life has always been cheap in Mexico.

"What is your name, *muchacho?*" Parra asked.

Doroteo hesitated, then said, "Pancho Villa!"

Parra laughed uproariously, but Doroteo was serious. "You mean," Parra said, "the great *bandido* of many years ago."

"His namesake," Doroteo lied.

From that moment on Doroteo Arango lived under the name of Francisco (Pancho) Villa. What prompted him that day to assume the name of a long-deceased Mexican outlaw was never explained by him. The name stuck. In later years, when close friends referred to him as Doroteo Arango, he showed resentment. It was another of his unexplained vagaries.

In 1914 Pancho Villa and some members of his staff were royally entertained at a banquet in El Paso by a group of Border Babbitts, Army officials, dyspeptic merchants and shirt-tail politicians. There was much falderol, strained gaiety and brave repartee during the dinner courses.

Women in dazzling evening gowns, diplomats in uncomfortable tails, and army men embued with the Wilsonian doctrine of goodwill, all strove discreetly for Villa's favor. What did it matter if Pancho, donned in the uniform he despised, had spilt some soup on his jacket front? Or if he preferred to sit and munch candy instead of partake of the dessert?

Pancho Villa was the man of the hour in Mexico. The erudite President Wilson, aware of Villa's power, was handling the Mexican badman with silk glove diplomacy. Word was momentarily expected in El Paso that Washington, weary of its neighbor's turbulence, had chosen the lesser of several evils and had agreed to recognize the Villa government.

Much to the distress of the diners, an American newspaperman, flush with champagne, disregarded decorum and hailed Villa for an interview.

"I hear," blurted the renegade reporter, "your real name is Doroteo Arango, *Señor.*"

"My name is Pancho Villa," said Villa.

"And you don't smoke or drink?"

Villa shook his head, still munching candy.

"You must have *some* redeeming faults, *Señor*," said the facetious newsman.

"I do," Villa replied. "Women. I am what you *Americanos* call a son of a bitch when it comes to women. But I'd call you one, *Señor*, without women."

A few people remember, still nervously, how narrowly an "international incident" was averted that night. Today the erstwhile newspaperman operates a cantina in Matamoros. He could, of course, if so inclined, be writing for radio.

"Despite his deep yen for banditry," Otis Aultman once said, "Pancho was one of the most completely honest men I ever knew. He robbed with charming finesse. If he owed you money he'd pay it — in all probability by robbing some one else. Love of money was certainly never one of his sins. Money to him was only the means of attaining something else. At one time he had millions, and flung it to the winds like confetti."

Bandit chieftain Parra accepted Pancho as a member of his band without further ado. Something about the youth's brash candor and swagger appealed to the older out-trailers. More than that, as a neophyte into outlawry, he immediately displayed a tremendous aptitude for the holdup game.

Fate played a strange hand on the first "job" in which Pancho participated. Plans were carefully laid to rob the Mexican Mining Company's stage of its $100,000 payroll; but plans sometimes go awry in holdups. Instead of the stage carrying its usual guards, suspecting mine officials jammed the inside of the vehicle with Federal soldiers.

As the outlaws pounced down upon the coach, it seems that all unshirted hell broke loose. Several of the outlaws were killed before they got the situation — and the payroll money — in hand. Among those to die was Chieftain Parra. But during the fracas, Pancho shot, rode and issued orders with such gusto and agility that his future leadership was assured.

If any of the more seasoned members of the dead Parra's band resented the blazing-eyed upstart's leadership, it was never revealed. Also, it is interesting to note that three members of this original fraternity stayed with Pancho from that day through the many years of bloody revolution. They were Tomas Urbina, Martin Lopez and Juan Salas.

The next twelve years of Pancho Villa's life does, undeniably, assume a piquant Robin Hood flavor. Still, there were brutal atrocities committed that taint the flavor. Whether his sanguinary deeds overshadowed his acts of benevolence is purely a matter of personal opinion.

Why search back through the haze of time and yellowed records for reasons to justify Villa's acts? To me it always has been faintly amusing to watch the pained expressions on the faces of moralists who decry murder but who condone war.

At this period of Pancho's life his sole motive was one of vengeance. He and his men had no "Cause" to point to for justification of their unsavory acts. Villa had his first taste of power; his promptings were atavistic. He lashed out at the *hacendados*, the Spanish dons and the wealthy aristocrats with the fury of a man obsessed. The bull-whip scars on his back still pained him. He wanted revenge.

After assuming leadership of the outlaw band, one of his first moves was to return to the Hacienda Rio Grande to see his mother. He returned in the dead of night. His pockets bulged with his share of the Mexican Mining Company loot. His mother, brothers and sisters embraced him tearfully.

Top: Bodies of dead men on a side street in Jimenez immediately after the town was captured by Villa.

Below: Mass hangings were commonplace. Traitors and men disloyal to Villa were promptly hanged from the nearest cottonwood limb.

"My son," his mother sobbed. "Each day and night I have prayed for your safety. Tell me what has happened. Where did you get this wealth of money?"

The tough young outlaw grinned, though his eyes were wet with tears. He dumped the money on a table, saying, "It is yours, Mother. From now on you and the children will live well —"

"But. Doroteo —"

"I have a job that pays much money, Mother. This is what I have saved. Remember, I always said I would take you away from this life of slavery."

Before dawn next morning, Pancho rode safely away from the ranch, not knowing it would be the last time he would see his mother alive. By artful lying he kept the truth of his outlawry from her. Why she stayed on at the ranch and sent the children to live in Chihuahua City has never been explained.

Pancho's next return to the ranch brought with it a shock that he told about to only one man—Jose Jaurrieta. These are Pancho's exact words, translated from Spanish:

"Imagine my horror when I entered the house and saw my mother lying on the bed, dead. Tapers were burning, and there were mourners in the room, but I didn't see them. So absorbed was I in my grief I dropped to my knees at the bedside and kissed one of mother's hands. I was crying like a baby when I heard voices outside the room calling for help and saying, 'Catch him! Catch him! It's Doroteo.'

"Kissing my dead mother for the last time I hurriedly left the room. With a pistol in each hand I fought my way to my horse. In the squabble I killed two men."

In the years that followed Pancho gained full stature as an outlaw. Mostly his nefarious operations were in the State of Chihuahua, where he came to know the far-flung deserts, the sheer-walled, isolated canyons of the mountains where an army of men could find safe refuge from the blundering searches of the Federal troops.

Pancho delighted in playing hide and seek with the law. Life to him was a Game. He grew more daring with each passing year, recruiting more men to his band, smashing out at *hacendados* with increasing fury. The American Smelting & Refining Company and El Potosi Mining Company, big operations in Chihuahua, felt the sting of his depredations.

The vast, feudal estate of the mighty Don Luis Terrazas suffered from cattle losses and property damage that drove the Señor Terrazas into a frenzied, white-faced rage. In helpless fury the kingly Don tried to halt the scourge by recruiting an army of his own; but in the eyes of his *peon* troopers the Villa rampages were acts of gallantry. Secretly they admired the daring Pancho. Was not Villa robbing the rich and giving to the poor?

The story of Don Luis Terrazas is worthy of a volume in itself. It is a saga as rich in fantasy as "Alice In Wonderland," as imperiously chivalric as Henry the Eighth's court, as tragic as a Teutonic legend. In northern Mexico, prior to 1912, his empire consisted of thousands of acres, including towns and remote villages. His word was law; he owned fabulously rich mines. His cattle herds defied counting, as did the *peones* whose lives he controlled.

The great Don's hacienda was rich with the furnishings of Old Spain. His art treasures alone were worth millions. He entertained royally, with all the pomp of a Ceasar. His ladies rode in a gold-trimmed carriage pulled by dazzling white horses. The vainglorious rule of this proud, dignified dandy prods even the most vivid imagination.

Once, one of the large Chicago packing plants wired Don Luis, asking him if it would be possible for him to supply them immediately with 15,000 head of beef cattle. The imperious Don wired back: "WHAT COLOR?"

But no desert storm equals the fury and devastation of a country in the throes of a bloody revolution. Don Luis lived to see his land confiscated, his multitude of *peones* rebel, his wealth usurped — by Villa. Don Luis escaped, a broken, bitter old man, to El Paso, Texas. His eldest son died as a result of Villa's torture.

In El Paso Don Luis once stood on the front porch of his home and watched the Villa forces drive his cattle from out of the hills to the Juarez slaughter house pens. Don Luis' health was gone; death was soon to claim him. But in those last days of anguish his soul cried out with all the bitter torment a man can know.

A few years ago I bought the old Terrazas home in

El Paso, and lived there. Though no psychic manifestations were ever in evidence, one had the uncomfortable sensation at times that the Don's ghost was following one through the creaky halls, still declaiming his wrath against Villa in whispered monotones.

But back to Villa and out with the spiritual didoes. That Pancho did rob the rich and help the poor is indisputable. He raided villages, smashed down store fronts, and told the hungry *peones* to cart off all the food and supplies they wanted. He kidnapped influential, wealthy citizens, and held them for king-sized ransoms.

Pancho Villa! The name swept the country. It gained an aura of magic. To the men of position and wealth the name was anathema; to the *peon* it was his spark of hope for salvation. Newsmen north of the Rio Grande clung to the lurid Villa tales and shouted joyously, "Brother, he's good copy!"

There was drama in Villa's movements: dust and the thunder of racing hoofs, the lusty cries of defiance from the throats of his men, blood and excitement — and always the unexpected. His outlaw band swelled as *peones* threw down their hoes and joined him.

Frantic cries for help were heard in far off Mexico City. The hell-for-leather forays of this Pancho Villa were no shoot-and-run affairs. In Washington, a rotund President Taft cocked an ear to the rumblings, shook free of his inertia, and kept the wires humming to the American ambassador in Mexico City.

Villa's trumpeting vengeance shouts were suddenly lost in the rising clamor for rebellion. Millions of *peones,* galling under the yoke of Diaz tyranny, began a chant of unrest that was soon to rise to thunderous proportions — and to ten years of revolution.

Word came out of Mexico City that President Porfirio Diaz was on his death-bed. Since 1876 he had guided the destiny of Mexico with an iron hand. He was past his eightieth year. He had been an Empire builder; he had developed the country's natural resources, built railroads and encouraged foreign investments. But from his dictatorial heights he had forgotten the human element: that millions of *peones* were starving in a land of plenty.

Rumors flew like wildfire. Plots and counter-plots were hatched overnight. Mexican intrigue — as only the Latins know it — was rampant. "Death to Diaz!" chanted the mob in front of Chapultepec Castle. In a side-street cantina, General Victoriano Huerta, the inscrutable Indian, was in conclave with other powerful army officials.

General Huerta, over his *copitas*, listened quietly to the fawning solicitations of his underlings that he take over the reins of government. He was playing a cautious game, ever conscious of the mob's fickleness. Diaz had made Huerta what he was; Huerta had sworn loyalty to the ailing monarch. But Huerta coveted the *presidente's* job. He'd wait for the propitious moment, then ride to power on the tide.

In El Paso a mild-mannered little man, who called himself The Redeemer, and who spoke with such evangelical fervor as to enlist a following, claimed that all of the State of Chihuahua was back of him. And, politically speaking, as Chihuahua State goes, so goes Mexico.

This pint-sized patriot was named Francisco I. Madero. He had visited President Diaz a few months before, and urgently requested the dictator to dismount his throne. He had spoken so eloquently and with such sincerity that Diaz listened enraptured, forgetting to dispatch a messenger for his firing squad.

It seems that Madero's visionary diatribe rose to such spellbinding heights of double-talk that the old dictator was flabbergasted. He did manage to ascertain that Madero was in favor of a Utopian democracy of sorts, wherein all the Mexican people were to live in ethereal bliss.

"And who," Porfirio demanded, "could possibly do all this for Mexico — were I to abdicate?"

"I could," said the modest Madero, and walked out — miraculously safe.

In the face of this cyclonic furore, Villa, from his secluded aerie, peered off in the direction of Chihuahua City and let his thoughts turn to love. During all these years of his buccaneering he had never forgotten Luz Corral. He had on numerous occasions, with swashbuckling gallantry, kept secret appointments with her. Just how ardent was Villa's love-making at these rendezvous is a matter for speculation. But the sincerity of his heart-tug for the loyal ever patient, plump little Luz can never be denied.

In later years, when other love-yearnings carried him

far afield, he consistently returned to Luz, his first wife. He consorted with other women — women of exotic beauty and breeding, barroom trollops, and seductive adventuresses; and he held these consorts with such a show-window display of naivete that the stunned moralists could at first only sputter.

Villa was to marry three other women beside Luz. Three are recorded. Perhaps there were more. He had children by them. There were, naturally, intra-family jealousies, hair-pullings and screamed threats; but when these tornadic brawls threatened of mayhem, Villa walked away from the with the charming indifference of a full-fed bull in a pasture.

The complicated laws of marriage and divorce, to Villa, were like an Einsteinian calculus problem to a small child: he never understood them. The ritual and ceremony of a church wedding were boresome. He saw a woman; he wanted her. What other rite was necessary than for him to say: "You're my wife now. Here is some money. I'll see that you get more. Remember, there's nothing I hate worse in life than an unfaithful woman."

Luz Corral and Pancho were married by a padre October 17, 1909, in the small town of San Andres, near Chihuahua City. It was a brief ceremony, attended by the bride's parents and a few select friends, all of whom kept one eye cocked for the police. The girl's parents had bravely consented to her marriage with the hell-raising fugitive; they had no other choice.

"I was the only woman that Pancho really loved," says Luz Corral de Villa.

4.

Comet In The Sky

HE next ten years of Mexican history takes on an operatic aspect, with Pancho Villa emerging from the wings, grizzled and unbathed, to ursurp the leading role with such gusto and charm that the audience sat momentarily entranced; then, as one, they rose to their feet, their hysterical cries of "bravo" shaking the rafters.

At times it was "above the pitch, out of tune, and off

the hinges," as Rabelais said. At times the warring actors, unknowingly, assumed the comic roles of a Gilbert and Sullivan masterpiece; again, it was a phantasmagoria of flashing knives and gunshots, when the players, completely off their lines, shouted to be heard. There were moments of Lydian measures from the orchestra; then the shocking crescendo of crashing cymbals and kettle drums. But Pancho held to his leading role until his curtain fell with an ignominious crash.

Of this period the late Bill Greet used another analogy "It was a game of chess, with death the only stake. All the players involved—Diaz, Huerta, Madero, Orozco, Carranza, Villa and the kibitizers—they all died tragically. It was a game of such swift fury and treachery it takes a score-board, a mathematician and a score of Philadelphia lawyers to arrive at any kind of a conclusion as to the winner."

After his marriage, Pancho got word by the grapevine of Francisco Madero's uprising in the State of Chihuahua. With a rag-tag army, Madero already had captured such towns as Guerrero, Janos, Cerro Prieta and Mal Paso. The tide was turning in his favor. He was a dreamer, a spiritualist, a crystal ball gazer. He was a Messiah, a man with a Message. His beard resembled a Biblical prophet's outcropping. His dark eyes were soft and lustrous, filled with visions.

This Francisco I. Madero was only thirty-three years of age at the time. Born of aristocratic parents in the State of Coahuila, he had studied at one of the larger universities, but his rabid reform utterances cut short his academic days. His advocacy of the Diaz regime overthrow sent him to jail. He spent years behind the bars, finally escaping across the border to San Antonio, Texas.

In languid San Antonio no great furore was caused when the dignified Madero, October 10, 1910, issued a manifesto to the effect that President Diaz was a dictator and a scoundrel. A little more than a month later he proclaimed himself the Provisional President of Mexico. He brought his Message, his charm and promises to El Paso, and won the populace to his Cause.

He recruited a small army; he promised the enslaved masses of Mexico an earthly paradise. Moral support of Texas was assured; also rifles and ammunition by surreptitious river crossings. Madero was a "natural", and knew it.

A spell-binder, but no soldier, Madero turned his army

manuevering over to a Pascual Orozco, a tall, grim-faced revolutionist — a complete opposite to Madero. General Orozco was tough and cruel; human life to him was dirt cheap. He was a dangerous foe, ready always to change political affiliations when the chance for personal betterment offered itself.

Further tidings came to Villa that were to change his entire career. The report was that Don Abran Gonzales, a man of sterling character, now Provisional Governor of the State of Chihuahua, was supporting Madero.

Pancho had heard of Don Abran's trustworthiness. He began doing some deep thinking. His life as a bandit was fast losing its glamor. He was tired of constantly being hunted by bounty-grabbers. His marital life was a kiss-and-run affair that no woman could tolerate long.

Did Villa's wife, Luz Corral, exert a woman's influence and plead with him to make a change? Perhaps. But no woman's charms influenced him too greatly. Villa, still seeking vengeance against the ruling class, realized that if he could join the Madero-Gonzales faction, *he would be continuing his own fight under the protective flag of a Cause.*

Let no charitable historian imply that Villa, because of an overwhelming patriotic fervor, wished to join Madero. He, Villa, was far too earthily realistic for that. He was thinking of his own hide, his own welfare, his own fight against the wealthy.

Pancho sent an emissary to Don Abran Gonzales, offering the services of his outlaw band to the revolutionary cause. Surprisingly, Gonzales hurried back a message of enthusiastic acceptance. Men like the great Pancho were needed for The Cause. He would be a soldier now, not a bandit.

"I appoint you, by the authority vested in me," Governor Gonzales wrote, — "a Captain in the revolutionary forces."

With jubilation tempered by caution, Pancho and his men rode into Chihuahua City. Villa met Gonzales, and an instant friendship was formed. With genuine humility Pancho listened to the older man's advice and instructions. This eventful day was December 10, 1910. Villa was thirty-one years of age, but he looked older.

Gonzales spoke with high praise of their leader, Francisco Madero. "I like you, *Señor* Villa, despite the fact that you are branded a killer and an outlaw. Society has made you what you are. I know you hate Diaz and all he stands for. Now is your chance to fight on the side of right. We want to free the enslaved masses of our country. We want equality — a democracy like the *Americanos* have . . . ."

Villa listened. For the first time in his life a great man was talking to him, as an equal.

"I know," Villa mumbled. "I know. And believe me, *Señor* Gonzales, I shall never forget this day. I know the torture and hopelessness of being a slave, for I've been one. I'll fight, or die if need be, for the revolution's success."

Pancho had a Cause.

He and his men were directed to report to General Orozco, Commander of the Revolutionary forces. Orozco took one look at the unkempt Villa and his forty men, and greeted them coldly. He had heard of Villa, the outlaw.

An instant enmity was born between Orozco and Villa. It may be that in Villa the revolutionary commander saw a man destined to go places.

Villa said later, "In General Orozco's eyes all I could see was treachery."

Orozco had no choice but to accept Villa and his men as soldiers of the revolution. Villa at this time did not organize his famed Dorados as is sometimes claimed. Not until 1913, in the town of Ascension, State of Chihuahua, did Villa conceive the idea of organizing his "Golden Ones."

The meeting of Villa and Francisco Madero was a memorable one for Pancho. The little man of illusions and dreams, Madero, barely came to the thick-shouldered Pancho's chest. He addressed Villa politely, warmly; his Spanish was faultless. He had the credulous charm of a small child, the intellect of an Oxford professor, the energy of a powerful turbine.

"It made me feel good when Madero treated me like a man of his own equal," Villa said. "I would gladly have died for him then and there. I loved him like a father."

No people on earth love a parade like Mexicans. For hours they will stand in the scorching sun, docile and patient, waiting for the banners and bands to pass. No other people, once aroused, flock so fervently to a Cause. Religious by nature, volatile and passionate, sentimental and kind, trusting and courteous—they have all these attributes. But they must have a Cause. It is a fetish with them.

Top: A rare picture of Villa's crack Dorados. Villa is seen in bottom row, center.

Left: One of the few pictures taken of Villa wearing shirt, tie, civilian coat and vest.

Center: Floyd Gibbons, famous newspaper correspondent, standing alongside his Chicago Tribune box-car.

Right Center: Rodolfo Fierro, "The Butcherer," so named because of his love for executing prisoners.

Lower Left: Tough Americans who formed an outfit of their own to fight for Villa's Cause.

Lower Right: Attack on Torreon. Villa in center, surrounded by American newsmen and staff officers.

Madero gave them that Cause. And they responded with all the fire of religious fanatics. Pancho Villa—once the great *bandido*—was on their side. Pancho's legend grew; stories of his tiger-like courage, his valor and his defiance of the Diaz tyrants brought *peones* swarming to the colors.

The Revolution spread like a prairie fire. Juarez was alerted, and the people were in a state of near panic; street fighting was reported in Zacatecas, Gomez Palacio and Chihuahua City. All of Chihuahua State echoed to the hue and cry, *"Viva Madero! Muera Diaz!"* Rebels in Durango, Coahuila and parts of Sonora were on the march.

President Diaz, genuinely alarmed, issued peace feelers, fatuous and vague while parrying for time. His power and very life were teetering on the brink; the distant rumble of thunder held fearful tidings. At his back, smiling inscrutably, stood General Huerta.

In sporadic fighting Captain Villa distinguished himself as a hero. Where the dust, din and bullets were thickest — there was Pancho, six-shooter spewing death, his brown teeth flashing beneath his untrimmed mustache. In Chocolate Pass, March 19, 1911, he and his men completely routed the Federalistas, inflicting heavy losses.

American newsmen, intrigued by Pancho the firebrand, came running. They liked Villa and disliked the colorless Orozco. Villa's devil-may-care swagger, his bawdy sense of humor appealed to them. He was good copy, any day. His language sparkled, like his eyes; his obscenities were uproarious. And General Orozco, disgruntled at his own second-fiddle accompaniment, looked on, hating Villa with all his heart.

The United States Government, alarmed lest the tide of battle might wash across the border, immediately sent twenty thousand troops to the El Paso district.

President Diaz, realizing his own doom now, thought only of abdication and escape. May 9, 1911, General Orozco ordered his troops to take Juarez, the key Mexican city opposite El Paso. Colonel Guiseppi Garibaldi, grandson of the Italian patriot, was in charge of the artillery. Villa, now promoted to a colonel, had his own renegade outfit which included many Americans.

In that group with Villa were such fire-eaters as Sam Dreben, Oscar Creighton and Tracy Richardson — all captains. Richardson had in his own command a group of

American cowboys. The way they captured the Juarez
bull-ring, whooped, shot, and rode hell-for-leather into the
thick of the battle is still remembered by El Pasoans who
stood atop buildings on the Texas side and shouted themselves hoarse.

The battle raged one day and a night. Dead bodies
littered the streets. Building fronts were smashed in and
houses wrecked by artillery fire. Stray bullets reached
El Paso killing several Americans. Then General Navarro,
Commander of the Juarez Garrison, surrendered uncon-
ditionally.

In Mexico City, at Buena Vista station, a tired, sad,
old tyrant closed his eyes to the glitter of the city he loved.
He wore his uniform bravely, but his eyes were filled with
tears. Grizzled, white-haired, the old exile held in fond
abrazo the only man he could trust.

"I came into power by a military coup, General Huerta,"
he said tiredly. "I go out the same way."

Huerta, the inscrutable Indian, smiled without mirth.
"You ruled Mexico wisely, *mi* General," replied Huerta.
"The screaming rabble will never be satisfied. They have
not the intelligence to rule themselves. Talk of democracy
in Mexico is the loose jabbering of fools."

"You are a man of Destiny, General Huerta," said
Diaz prophetically. "Mexico can be yours if you want it.
But I caution you: do not let my fate happen to you."

The exiled ruler and his family steamed out of Vera
Cruz two nights later aboard a liner bound for France.
Porfirio Diaz was going to his Saint Helena. He died in
Paris, July 2, 1915, a forgotten figure.

5.

The Storm Clouds Gather

HE first act was over for Villa. From the
shadows of the wings he had emerged, unwel-
comed by some of the other actors; but the
dazzling brilliance of his performance had won
the fancy of the audience. He had heard the
avalanche of applause and liked it.

With the affairs of state in the competent hands of

Madero and Gonzales, Villa hearkened to the love calls of Luz Corral. She was soon to present him with their first-born, a boy.

In mid-summer of 1911, Villa returned to Chihuahua City. The Diaz government was no longer existent. He was not a bandit now, but a war hero. He could live as other men, earn an honest living and enjoy family life.

But Villa's innate restlessness was not compatible to the drab existence of a family man. He had vine leaves in his hair; applause still echoed in his ears. Being non-allergic to blood, he opened a butcher shop, and prospered. One reason he prospered was because he was never known to buy a head of beef for slaughtering purposes.

If, during the dark hours of night, a rancher's prize beef disappeared, it was generally assumed that the fresh hide could be found in the rear of the Villa butcher shop next day. But no irate rancher ever deemed it advisable to question Villa about such a delicate matter.

In later years when questioned about this phase of the meat business, Villa would laugh uproariously. "Poor cows," he would say. "It didn't matter to them who they belonged to. Why should it matter to anyone else?"

In August, Abran Gonzales — Villa's *compadre* — was formally elected Governor of Chihuahua. With swift formality, after a brief *pro tem* reign by another man, Francisco Madero was duly inaugurated President of Mexico. He took office November 5, 1911.

Outwardly, Mexico's stormy days were past, but the lull that followed was a brief interlude to the chaos that was yet to come. Peace in a country once riled is a fickle thing. Madero surrounded himself with soft-stepping dreamers, like himself, who gazed at the stars in aesthetic delight, deafening themselves to the rumble of the approaching storm.

As a ruler Madero was a failure. His year and four months in office produced none of the Utopian bliss he had promised the laboring classes. His promises failed to materialize; he stood still when he should have been on the run.

The first major thunderbolt came with news that General Orozco, intent upon the overthrow of the Madero government, was in organized revolt. This was in March, 1912. Orozco got a following, claiming that Madero was spineless — a false prophet and a betrayer. Several towns in Chihuahua already had fallen to the Orozco troops.

Top: Villa, posing in uniform, sits for picture with another one of his wives.
Below: Colonel Guissepi Garibaldi and General Pascual Orozco.

Villa hastily laid aside his butcher knives and went to Mexico City to consult with the president. Madero received him warmly, accepted the erstwhile bandit's offer of help, and got in touch with Governor Gonzales. With customary vigor, Pancho returned to Chihuahua City, was summarily put in command of a large force of men, and went in search of the traitorous Orozco. He struck first at Parral, capturing the garrison and quieting things generally. Orozco and his men fled into the mountains.

Madero, still pacing the floor of his astral heights, ordered Villa to take his troops to Jimenez, Chihuahua; there Pancho was to report to General Huerta. Another uprising was rumored to be in the offing in that locale.

Huerta's game of waiting was still progressing. Behind thick-lensed glasses his black eyes masked his cruelty and cunning. He felt only contempt for Madero; but his hate for the uncouth Villa was a searing flame. Villa had won all the applause and had stolen the spotlight. Huerta fumed.

That meeting between Villa and General Huerta can best be described by Pancho himself. "Huerta and his staff officers did not get up from their chairs that morning I walked into headquarters. I was dusty and tired. All the men there were dressed in gala uniforms. But because I was not in the regular army I was wearing my usual old clothes.

"I never forgot the way those men looked me up and down as if I were a stray mongrel that smelled bad. My loyalty to the president was the only reason I was there, but right then I wished I had been miles away. Later, when Huerta had Madero assassinated, I lived from that moment on to square things with Huerta."

With no effort to disguise his feelings, Huerta assigned Villa and his cavalry to quarters. Tension mounted between the two leaders. Trouble was inevitable. But it came sooner than expected, all through Villa's inordinate love of horse-flesh.

A horse disappeared one night from a neighboring rancher's corral. Next day Villa was seen riding the animal. The indignant rancher loosed his wrath upon General Huerta. The seething Indian commander detailed some staff officers to arrest Pancho. *Andale!*

Villa exploded when the officers suggested arrest for his larceny. "This horse is mine!" Villa roared. "You sniveling bastards can go to hell . . . . and take Huerta with you!"

He was still charging the welkin with unprintable phrases as the officers stalked off. That night he was sleeping soundly when a detail of soldiers roused him. The troopers' guns were cocked and leveled. They were taking no chances with the man who could wield a butcher knife with such dexterity.

"Come," said the officer in command.

Confronted by Villa, Huerta let loose a tirade that all but blistered the white-washed walls. Villa was given no chance to defend himself. "You have insulted me, Colonel Villa!" Huerta shouted darkly. "You are a common thief. The horse you have stolen is punishable by death . . . . and that's what it will be — death! You will be executed by a firing squad at five o'clock in the morning!"

The camp was stunned when the news spread of Huerta's verdict. Under heavy guard, Villa was imprisoned. What his emotions were that night, no one can know. In the darkness of his cell he stared into empty space. He loved life, but death held no horror for him.

What else happened that night assumes all the elements of a movie thriller, perfectly timed. In camp was Major Raoul Madero, the president's brother. The major was exceedingly fond of Villa; he knew that Villa was sometimes incorrigible, but the ex-butcher was loyal to the Madero Cause.

Major Madero secretly wired the president explaining the situation. No reply came back. Midnight came and passed. More anxious waiting. Another wire, frantic with appeal, sped on its way to the capital. Major Madero paced the floor, his face pale, drawn. Dawn was breaking. Then *click, click . . . . clickety-click . . . .*

Major Madero snatched the message from the telegraph operator. It was a reprieve for Villa from the president of Mexico. The major raced out to his horse, leaped astride.

Villa was standing in front of the execution wall. He had refused the blindfold. His head was held high, his eyes feverish with contempt for death. The firing squad members raised their rifles at a barked command. Just then up wheeled Major Madero, waving a telegram that saved Villa's life.

The incident that followed is one that commentators have related in many strange ways, and no two stories coincide. What happened was that Huerta, livid with frustration, forced Villa to crawl through the dust to where he stood near the firing squad. And in order to save his own life, Villa obeyed.

"It was the most humilating experience of my whole life," Villa said later.

In El Paso, years after, the dying Huerta spoke of this incident and said regretfully, "I should have killed Villa that day regardless of Madero's reprieve. It was one of the biggest mistakes I ever made."

Villa was taken to Mexico City and placed in the penitentiary instead of being shot. Here he had plenty of time for meditation. His thoughts were far from languid love dreams about Luz Corral. Night and day he thought of one thing: how he could kill General Huerta.

He worked with avid patience, while another actor entered the scene. This man was Carlos Juaregui, Clerk of the Military Court. He and Villa became close friends; they had long secretive talks. From a mysterious source, Villa got money — more than enough to buy favors. This money unquestionably came from the Maderos.

At high noon one day Villa, his mustache shaved off, walked boldly out of the penitentiary. Certain guards turned their heads. At the railroad yards Villa met his cohort, Juaregui. They climbed aboard a freight train and went into hiding. Upon arrival in Chihuahua City they hid in the homes of some political friends. The Huerta faction raged: *Get Villa, dead or alive!*

In Juarez Villa found a friend who helped smuggle him across the line into El Paso. South El Paso has always been called "Little Chihuahua". It is a district of shabby tenements, dark alleys and blaring honkytonks, cheap hotels and brothels, squalor, pestilence, beggars, half-naked urchins and eyesore facades.

Here is poverty at its worst, life at its ugliest, and death a surcease from travail. The population is mostly Mexican; there are a few Chinese and Greeks. At nights the lighted store fronts reveal a motley stream of humanity along the walks. Cries of hawkers rise above the strident undertone of traffic. From a sagging balcony a child wails fitfully, a mother scolds. In a gloomy stairway a hollow-eyed girl with lips too red smiles at a passing boy; she speaks suggestively. He nods and follows her. In another doorway the bedraggled figure of a man stirs, lifts his head, mumbles his sneers.

Little Chihuahua! Hotbed for years of Mexican intrigue and an incubatory of Mexican revolutions—a sanctuary of the damned, a hide-out for political refugees, a melting pot of restless, stirring, sweaty humanity.

A tourist steps out the front door of the elegant Paso del Norte Hotel. He faces El Paso Street. Three blocks south is Little Chihuahua. He looks off in that direction. The Chamber of Commerce winces. *We're fixing to clean up that squalor,* a man says. The visitor smiles; he heard the same thing in El Paso thirty years ago.

In the dingy, odorous hallways of a Little Chihuahua "hotel" a heavy-shouldered Mexican with burning eyes asked a frowsy witch of a woman for a room. She eyed him with unveiled suspicion, this landlady of garlic aroma.

"You have money?" she demanded, in Spanish.

The man nodded.

"You'll have to sign the record. It's the law, and the police are not to be tampered with. Pay me now in advance. And what did you say your name was, mister?"

The man said quietly, "Doroteo Arango."

No preening dowagers, mindful of El Paso's social whirl, sought out the colorful Pancho with gilt-edged invitations to attend the glittering balls and banquets of a gay city. Lost in the squalor of South El Paso, he was at the low-tide ebb of his erratic career. He was an outcast, a fugitive from the blood-red turbulence of his own country.

January 13, 1913, the *El Paso Times* carried the following brief news item: "All doubts as to the whereabouts of Colonel Pancho Villa, the federal volunteer army officer who recently escaped from prison in Mexico City, where he had been placed for insubordination on orders from General V. Huerta, were removed last night when he was located in a South El Paso street rooming house by a *Times* reporter.

"Villa would not talk for publication. He said he did not care to discuss his escape from the penitentiary, nor would he tell how he crossed the border. At his room in the hotel were four bodyguards stationed at various places about the house. When seen by the *Times* representative, Villa was armed with two revolvers and a large dirk."

If, however, Villa's sudden appearance in El Paso

caused little disturbance in police and social circles, his snow-balling eminence in Mexico was under way. The tide of prominence was suddenly to turn and miraculously lift him to breath-taking heights.

Always about Villa was the aura of mystery. His cloak-and-dagger escape from the penitentiary enhanced that mystery. In smelly squalor, he was dramatic. He sent and received strange messages; his contacts with the "higher ups" in Mexico were common knowledge. "Things" were happening; no one knew for sure quite what.

Villa watched the events in Mexico City from afar, but nonetheless keenly. His love for Madero bordered on adulation. His hate for Huerta, Orozco and his "Red Flaggers" was like a horrible disease eating away at him. He made sudden and mysterious trips to Los Angeles, always reappearing in one of the lowlier dives in South El Paso.

Pancho learned to speak a smattering of English; his penned signature took on the Spencerian flourishes of an artist. He was not a drinker, but he would sip beer and watch amusedly as others got thick-tongued. And, except for an occasional cigarette puff, he avoided tobacco.

"Pancho never seemed to have *time* to smoke or drink," Manuel Gonzales said. "But let a woman smile at Pancho and he would cavort around like a lewd colt."

Pancho's sudden appearance in a side-street barroom charged the place with as much excitement—possibly more —than if Saint Augustin had walked in to the accompaniment of blaring trumpets. Men trailed after him, hopeful of a nod or a smile. He bought drinks promiscuously, waving at the mob; he swaggered; he hinted of esoteric happenings; he flashed much money. And the Mexicans of South El Paso went wild, their hysterical cries for the great Pancho rising to monstrous reverberations.

Nor were the Mexicans in El Paso alone in this hue and cry. In Chihuahua, in Mexico City and far-off Coahuila, the enslaved masses shouted the magic name. They were tired of Madero; they hated Huerta; they scoffed at the colorless Orozco. They wanted Villa! Villa, who was a one time slave! Villa, who knew how to fight and kill, the Mexican way! Ah, *Señor*, they cried, he can save Mexico; he will give us food to fill our bellies; he is brave and daring . . . .

In Mexico City a weary, nerve-tense American Ambas-

Top Left: Victoriano Huerta, one-time president of Mexico, who fled from the country, later dying in El Paso, Texas.

Top Right: Villa conferring with an unidentified staff officer.
Below: Bodies strewn along street in Parral after one of the many revolutionary battles.

sador was in constant touch with Washington. The roaring revolutionary tornado was already in the outskirts of the Mexican Babylon. An American newspaper's headlines screamed: 5 MILLION ROUNDS OF AMMUNITION SHIPPED INTO REPUBLIC FROM U. S.

Washington favored Madero, distrusted Huerta, and chose to ignore the clamor for Villa. Senator William Alden Smith, Chairman of the Senate Committee investigating Mexican affairs, let go a broadside: "Approximately 5 million rounds of ammunition have been shipped from New Orleans to Mexico since the neutrality proclamation was issued by President Taft last spring. It appears that the Madero faction in Mexico has been permitted to get unlimited quantities of arms and ammunition, while his opponents have been forced to comply with the president's proclamation."

But Washington kept thumbs down on Huerta, flatly promising him no recognition if he came into power. There were even dark hints of intervention, and subtle political jabs that infuriated Huerta to the point of fiery denunciation. Warnings flew thick and fast. Washington had stuck out its proverbial neck; there was no pulling it back now.

One incensed editorialist, a prenatal internationalist, raged: "We shall send our soldiers into Mexico, if need be. American and English investments, as well as lives, must be protected . . . ."

The storm broke overnight, frightful in its fury, terrifying in its devastation. For exactly a fortnight it raged, starting February 10, 1913 and ending February 24. Headlines and front-page articles from the *El Paso Times* tell the story with admirable vigor.

Feb. 10, 1913:

ANOTHER REVOLT IN CITY OF MEXICO IS CHECKED BY THE BRAVERY OF PRESIDENT MADERO AND 1,000 LOYAL TROOPS NOW WITH HIM.

Feb. 11:

MADERO IS CONFIDENT OF VICTORY.

Feb. 12:

TERRIBLE STREET ARTILLERY DUEL RAGED ALL DAY YESTERDAY IN MEX CAPITAL.

FOUR ARMORED U. S. CRUISERS ORDERED TO FOUR PRINCIPAL MEX PORTS

These transports will receive troops, should further action be deemed necessary. The purpose merely is to take precautionary steps to protect Americans and foreigners in the City of Mexico, should conditions of violence continue and anarchy succeed.

The attitude of the government still is strongly against intervention and it was determined to take no step at this time which would commit us to such a policy, and to take only reasonable precautions to meet an exigency which is earnestly hoped and believed will not arise.

Feb. 14:

MEXICO CITY BATTLE CONTINUED ALL YESTERDAY WITHOUT BRINGING THE GENERALLY EXPECTED RESULTS.

PRESIDENT MADERO SAYS THE PROMISED CRUSHING BLOW WAS NOT DELIVERED FOR HUMANITARIAN REASONS; THE ENGAGEMENT YESTERDAY WAS CONTINUATION OF ARTILLERY DUEL WITH MUCH DESTRUCTION OF LIFE AND PROPERTY.

Feb. 15:

FEAR OF AMERICAN INTERVENTION HAS PROBABLY CAUSED VOLUNTARY RESIGNATION OF PRESIDENT MADERO.

Feb. 16:

PRESIDENT MADERO WILL DIE BEFORE HE WILL RESIGN.

Feb. 17:

MADERO'S MESSAGE TO PRESIDENT TAFT PLEADING AGAINST AMERICAN INTERVENTION.

Feb. 18:

FIGHTING CONTINUES IN MEXICO CITY WITHOUT APPARENT DECISIVE RESULTS.

PRESIDENT MADERO CERTAIN THAT VICTORY IS IN SIGHT.

GENERAL HUERTA TO BEGIN FLANK MOVEMENT IN WHICH HE WILL USE BOMBS AT SHORT RANGE. GEN. BLANQUET LOYAL AND PLACED IN COMMAND OF RESERVES AT NATIONAL PALACE.

Feb. 19:

MADERO IS FORCED TO RESIGN THE PRESIDENCY OF MEXICO THROUGH THE NEW PLOT FORMED MONDAY BY FEDERAL GENERALS BLANQUET AND HUERTA.

GEN. HUERTA PROCLAIMS HIMSELF PROVISIONAL PRESIDENT UNTIL GENERAL ELECTIONS ARE HELD.

ALL OF MADERO'S CABINET PLACED UNDER ARREST.

JOSE PINO SUAREZ, THE VICE PRESIDENT, WAS ARRESTED LAST NIGHT AND HELD PRISONER IN ANOTHER PART OF THE PALACE FROM WHERE MADERO WAS CONFINED.

Feb. 20:

GOV. OF TEXAS ON WARPATH REGARDING CONDITIONS ON THE BORDER.

JUAREZ DISLIKES NEW "PRESIDENT".

PRES. MADERO WILL BE EXILED BY MEXICAN MILITARY GOV.

GUSTAVO MADERO EXECUTED BY CAPTORS WEDNESDAY MORNING.

HUERTA CLAIMS MADERO ATTEMPTED HIS LIFE AND MAY PREVENT EXILE: MEXICAN CONGRESS SECRETLY ELECTS HUERTA PROVISIONAL PRESIDENT OF MEXICO.

Feb. 21:

MADERO'S ENEMIES FILE CHARGES IN ORDER TO HOLD HIM A PRISONER; ONE CHARGE FILED IS MURDER, ANOTHER DEPLETING TREASURY.

TERRAZAS WILL GET MILLIONS:

Friends of General Luis Terrazas, known as the "Rockefeller of Mexico" received word today that under the changed Mexican military administration, General Terrazas would be refunded lands and cattle valued at $20,000,000, and restored to his position of power in Mexico.

Feb. 22:

ANOTHER REVOLUTION HAS BROKEN OUT IN MEXICAN REPUBLIC IN OPPOSITION TO DEPOSING OF MADERO AND MILITARY RULE INSTITUTED BY CONSPIRATORS.

LOYAL MADERISTA GOVERNORS BUSY RAISING
TROOPS TO BATTLE FOR THE CONSTITUTIONAL
GOVERNMENT.
HUERTA ADOPTS PORFIRIO DIAZ POLICY.
U. S. INTERVENES TO SAVE FALLEN PRESIDENT.
Feb. 23: (Sunday)
MADERO AND SUAREZ TRANSFERRED FROM
PALACE TO PENITENTIARY; WIFE OF DEPOSED
PRESIDENT NOT ALLOWED TO SEE HIM.
Feb. 24:
(*El Paso Times* devoted entire front page to this story):
PRES. MADERO AND VICE PRESIDENT SUAREZ
WERE SHOT AND KILLED SATURDAY NIGHT IN
MEXICO CITY WHILE THEY WERE UNDER MILI-
TARY GUARD.

Francisco I. Madero and Jose Pino Suarez are
dead. In a midnight ride under guard from the
National Palace to the penitentiary they were
killed. The circumstances surrounding the death
of the deposed president and vice president of the
republic are unknown except as given in official
accounts which do not conform in all cases. The
only witnesses were those actually concerned in
the killing. The tragedy occured shortly after midnight. Madero and Suarez were placed in an automobile which was accompanied by another car and
escorted by a hundred rurales commanded by Com-
mandant Francisco Cardenas and Colonel Rafael
Pimiente.

With instructions not to outdistance the escort,
the cars moved slowly. No incident occurred until
they reached the point near the penitentiary, where
in an open place, the guards' attention was attract-
ed, according to the official version, to a group of
persons following. Shots were fired at the escort
out of the darkness.

The rurales closed in and ordered the prisoners
out of the car. Thirty of the guards surrounded
the prisoners, while the remainder disposed themselves to resist an attack. About fifty men, some

Ejército Constitucionalista
División del Norte

GENERAL EN JEFE

El Señor Miguel Zuburis, portador
de la presente, pasa a esa Ciudad para que te
sirvas entregarle la cantidad de DOS MIL PESOS
ORO $2000.

Chihuahua, Julio 24 de 1914.

El General En Jefe

[signature: Francisco Villa]

Señor Hipólito Villa

Ciudad Juárez

Ejército Constitucionalista
División del Norte

GENERAL EN JEFE

[signature]

He de agradecerte te sirvas entregarle al portador
de la presente, Sr. Adrián Solís, la suma de SIETE MIL QUINIEN
TOS DOLARES.

Chihuahua, Agosto 21 de 1914.

El General en Jefe.

[signature: Francisco Villa]

Al Sr. Hipólito Villa,

C. Juárez, Chih.

Letters from Villa to his brother, Hipolito Villa, authorizing money payments. Villa signed his name with flourishes, but was unable to write anything else.

```
Tabaco. . . . . . . . . .Gral. Villa -- encuentrase en
Mandeme ( ) kilos. . . . Tras ( ) hombres
Azucar. . . . . . . . . .Canuto Reyes
Puros. . . . . . . . . . Pablo C. Seanez
Cigarros. . . . . . . . .Calixto Contreras
Lunes. . . . . . . . . . Alrededores de Chihuahua
Martes. . . . . . . . . .    "      "     " Casas Grandes
Miercoles. . . . . . . .     "      "     " Villa Ahumada
Jueves. . . . . . . . . .    "      "     " Torreon
Viernes. . . . . . . . .     "      "     " Durango
Sabado. . . . . . . . . .    "      "     " Parral
Domingo. . . . . . . . . .   "      "     " San Buenaventura
Enero. . . . . . . . . . . Urgente
Febrero. . . . . . . . . . Necesita fondos
Marzo. . . . . . . . . . . Todo esta bien
Amigo. . . . . . . . . . . Avanza hacia
Licores. . . . . . . . . . Obregon
Naranjas. . . . . . . . . . Gavira
Limon. . . . . . . . . . . Luis Herrera
Mango. . . . . . . . . . . Jacinto Trevino
Platano. . . . . . . . . . Elias Calles
Capulin. . . . . . . . . . Sonora
Calabaza. . . . . . . . . . Carranza
Boniato. . . . . . . . . . Pablo Gonzales
Cuidado. . . . . . . . . . Trenes de pasajeros corren cada
No hay cuidado. . . . . . Trenes de carga corren cada
Libros. . . . . . . . . . Solamente corren trenes militares hasta
Nueces. . . . . . . . . . rifles -- carabinas -- pistolas
tinteros. . . . . . . . . parque
Lapices. . . . . . . . . . Urge conteste esta via
Maiz. . . . . . . . . . . El Paso, Texas
Cebada. . . . . . . . . . New Orleans
Judias. . . . . . . . . . Habana
Estupido. . . . . . . . . Consul Carrancista
Guayaba. . . . . . . . . . Comuniques con Gral. Villa


a-r       e-g       i-k       m-l       q-n       u-p       y-s
b-f       f-a       j-e       n-t       r-y       v-w       z-m
c-q       g-c       k-b       o-i       s-x       w-u
d-z       h-d       l-h       p-j       t-o       x-v
```

Top: Another letter from Pancho to his brother, Hipolito. Villa signed the note, but the body of the message was written by one of his officers. Below: The secret code used by Villa for transmitting military messages. This was made from the original.

afoot and some mounted, threw themselves upon the detachment guarding the cars and the exchange of shots lasted 20 minutes, when the attacking party fled. The dead bodies of Madero and Suarez were found.

Reports of the murder of Madero and Suarez reached Huerta in a matter of minutes. It is said he spent the night drinking *copitas,* smiling and jesting with intimate *politicos.* Behind his thick-lensed spectacles his black eyes were feverish with new plans. Had not Diaz called him a man of Destiny? He had never liked Madero. What did it matter if the finger of murder-guilt pointed his way?

"Men," he said, "do not have the intelligence to guide themselves. They must be told, and led."

6.
Tiger of the North

 HE day after Madero's murder, Governor Abran Gonzales of Chihuahua was assassinated. Political tyrants in Mexico City, like checker players, were sacrificing men to make final victory complete.

With the fire-and-fall-back tactics of a fourth rate revolutionary, Orozco rushed into the spotlight with cries of allegiance for Huerta. And because of the untenable furore, Huerta, grasping at thin straws of support, accepted Orozco's alleged loyalty as *bona fide,* and sent his rag-tag army afield to quiet the rioting masses.

When word reached Villa of the deaths of Madero, Suarez and Gonzales, the ex-butcher raged and cursed and cried. When the storm of his passions had subsided he spoke in a voice husky with hate:

"Squaring accounts with Huerta is all that matters."

Again the desire for revenge was his motivation; and, as pointed out, he was not fighting *for,* but *against.*

February 27, 1913, Pancho vanished from El Paso as mysteriously as he had arrived there. Carlos Jauregui, his prison benefactor, went with him. West of El Paso, near the smelter, horses, supplies and other men were waiting for them in the high salt cedar that flanked the river. They crossed the Rio Grande that night, heading into the black-shadows of Chihuahua where fate was to play a strange hand. From the inky heavens peered down Villa's star, its twinkling radiance like a benediction. Thorny mesquite tore at the riders' pants legs as they rode through the chaparral at the toe of the Juarez mountains. They came to plowed fields and halted. Some of the men dismounted and stole up to a 'dobe hovel. The dim figure of a half-dressed man answered their furtive knock. There was whispered talk.

"Come," the *peon* was told. "Villa is waiting. He is to lead us. We are meeting at the dam outside Chihuahua City. Pancho will give us liberty and crush Huerta beneath his bootheel. Tell your old woman to pass the word on to other men. If you have a gun, get it and come."

The man was back inside the house but a moment. He kissed his wife, his sleeping children. He was trembling with excitement; his eyes were those of a man mesmerized. He was caught in the spell. The great Pancho needed him! What did it matter if he suffered and died? Life now was a living hell.

"*Viva Villa!*" he cried fervently.

He came running to join the waiting group. He had a horse and a rifle. What else he needed, Villa would furnish. His ecstacy was a religious experience. The night seemed to echo the vibrant, thrilling, soul-stirring whisper: *Viva Villa!*

The group rode on, adding to their numbers at each 'dobe *jacal* and scattered village. At the head of the cavalcade rode Villa, grim-faced and silent. The tide had turned; in a few short months he was to become dictator of the State of Chihuahua, then all of Mexico, in one of the most incredible handsprings into prominence the world has ever seen.

In exactly three weeks after his El Paso exodus, Villa had an army of three thousand men, mounted and heavily armed. Chihuahua City was his goal, but with Orozco firmly entrenched there under the Huerta banner, Villa struck at smaller towns — and won them to his side.

In Mexico City, Huerta waited, angry but confident, finding surcease from worry by bottle-tippling. It galled him no end because the new *presidente* of the United States, Woodrow Wilson, refused to recognize him as Mexico's ruler; but he masked his wrath, referring to Wilson as "a great man of much intelligence."

Events now began happening with the rapid-fire outburst of a Gatling gun. The towns of Parral, Jimenez and Torreon fell before Villa's onslaughts. He converted or killed. He and his men rode like Apaches possessed, and fought like demons. Men flocked to the Villa Cause, shouting and singing. He was a demi-god, cursed by his enemies, idolized by the masses. Again American newspapers front-paged him in screaming headlines. Newsmen, caught by his glamor, made of him a Robin Hood, a sweat-stained knight with lofty ideals, a Sir Galahad with outlandish manners, a heller with the women, a military genius, a one-man army, a purveyor of lewd stories, and God's gift to Mexico.

But Villa was not alone in the revolutionary field. In the State of Coahuila, a man named Venustiano Carranza had recruited an army against Huerta. Carranza, fifty-four years of age at the time, was tall and compactly built. He had served as governor of his home state; he was a man of affluence and wealth. Although wealthy by inheritance, and a *hacendado*, he had been devoted follower of Madero.

Carranza was a man of much academic intelligence; he had not the dreams of Madero, nor the cunning of Huerta; but he was a schemer, a politician. His iron-grey mustachios and patriarchal beard lent impressiveness to his austere posing. Behind steel-rimmed spectacles his eyes could glare; but he practised the amenities of courtly behavorism.

To Carranza, Pancho was crude, obscene, primitive. He disliked Villa passionately; he was bitterly jealous of Villa's favor with the American press — of Pancho's popularity with the unpredictable *gringos*.

Carranza, terming himself "First Chief of the Constitutionalist Army," however, was too astute a politician to display his true feelings. He wrote Villa, beseeching the ex-butcher to join him. Pancho wrote back a crackling refusal that rolled back the dignified Carranza's scalp.

With a mighty effort to control himself, Carranza visited Pancho in Parral. He scolded Villa for cold-bloodedly executing Huerta officers and soldiers; he decried the atrocities laid to Villa. He, Carranza, didn't condone the plundering and thieving enjoyed by the Villa men. Couldn't he, Villa, realize that such horrendous acts would eventually bring down the wrath of the United States upon them? And they needed the *gringos* good will; also *gringo* guns, bullets and money.

Consider the Great Cause, harped Carranza.

Villa laughed, belched, and walked away.

Carranza fumed and pouted. The only help he could depend upon now would come from Alvaro Obregon, a fiery-tempered young revolutionist whose views coincided with the disgruntled Carranza.

The next two years were to see Villa's star glitter with a brilliance that dazzled the entire world. It is an era of nightmarish fact that reads like absurb fiction; it is a stage set wherein all the actors go berserk and start fighting among themselves, unmindful of the rioting audience, until Villa grabs the prompt book and spotlight, restores order, and is bowled overy by the down-crashing curtain.

It is a tableau of dirt and blood, of intrigue and treachery, of laughter and tears. Indeed, it was a spectacle of such outlandish grotesqueries and paradoxes and contradictions that it is little wonder the historians become confused. Battle followed battle in such swift procession as to bewilder a mathematical wizard.

But wherever there was something happening, there was Villa. His sense of the dramatic and theatrical timing were an innate gift. As a military strategist he gained recognition as a genius; his every move was swift, daring. He did the impossible. He shattered Mexican tradition by fighting at night and disregarding siestas.

He was unpredictable as a tornado, and just as devastating. If he was a murderer, cruel and sadistic, he was also, at times, a maudlin sentimentalist. He had his vices and his virtues; he was a paradoxical paragon. But always he was a great actor.

Because of his ferocity he was called "The Tiger Of The North." His battle strategy was often elemental, but it brought results. Prior to the bloody battle of Torreon, Villa called in his staff officers for a conference. Various opinions concerning battle plans were discussed by the men; they began haggling, each trying to impress Pancho with his own knowledge of military warfare.

Villa sat in silence, amused. Then he rose like a great stevedore, his eyes stabbing the group. *"Compañeros,"* he said acidly, "tomorrow we take Torreon. Each of you have your own ideas of attack. Tomorrow morning we shall all meet at seven o'clock in the city square. Those of you who are not there will be executed. That is all."

Next morning at seven o'clock, Pancho put in his appearance at the city square. The shooting had stopped. His staff officers were there, waiting. They had been there since six o'clock.

Several years ago a *viejo* who called himself *Perro Negro* — Black Dog — was care-taker of the Juarez graveyard. This gnome-like guardian of the graves, toothless and crippled, hobbled along on a wooden leg like a tired centipede. His wizened face was the shriveled mask of a pirate; his bloodshot eyes mirrored gore and tragedy. But with all his shocking physical aspects, *Perro Negro* was kind. His smile and politeness were those of a third-rate mortician. He liked to talk.

November 14, 1913, Villa first captured Juarez with hardly a shot being fired. He struck like lightning. At midnight a freight train, on schedule, wheezed into the station near the center of town. The station-master, wiping sleep from his eyes, took one look as the car doors flew wide, started to yell, then dropped dead from a single shot.

Villa's Dorados swarmed out of the box cars. They swept over the town like flood waters from a broken dam. Federal soldiers at the garrison, taken completely by surprise, dropped their rifles and surrendered. Most of the Federal officers, believing Villa to be two hundred miles away, were enjoying themselves in a main street cantina, drinking themselves to victory. They were captured with all the formality of Mexican politeness. Visiting El Pasoans left drinks untouched and headed for the international bridge like blatting sheep.

Within two hours the mopping up exercises were over. It was a rich haul for Villa; the bank vaults yielded much wealth; many of the prisoners were Villa traitors and political enemies who had caused the ex-Chihuahua butcher untold misery.

Pedro R. Gomez, called "The Dead Man", was a major in Villa's Dorados. He was wounded in battle 2 times, captured and executed with 5 shots, given the "grace" shot twice—one in forehead and one behind the ear—a total of 9 shots, all in one day, AND LIVED!

Top: One of the few pictures of Villa in uniform.
Below: "Battle of the Ditch Bank" outside Juarez. Man crouched in center of picture is Tracy Richardson.

At dawn, seventy-five of the prisoners — many of them high-ranking officers — were selected for execution. In the chill of early morning they were marched out to the graveyard. From building tops in El Paso the *Americanos* peered through field glasses, horrified. Along the Juarez streets the natives watched the death-processional in awed silence. It was war, they whispered. Men must die in war. They shrugged.

At the execution wall the prisoners, haggard and pale, lined up for death. There were no heroics among the doomed men. Most of them smoked. All of them refused the blindfold. They glanced at the rising sun; they looked at one another. Their scorn for death was superb.

One of them smiled wanly, said, "It will be warm today. I hope they bury us soon. I should hate to be bloated."

The firing squad formed. A straggling line of witnesses stood in the background, shaken and silent. Eyes brimmed with tears. One witness, convulsed with sobs, turned away and began to vomit.

From a group of officers suddenly stepped Villa. His heavy, round face was dark; his eyes were burning coals as he faced his captives.

One of the prisoners said, "I beg of you, *Señor* Villa—"

He got no further. In one of his maniacal tantrums, Villa screamed himself hoarse. "Shut up, you back-stabbing traitor! I don't want to hear your begging. You've lived off the fat of the land while we've starved. You're lice—dogs —sons of goats . . . . hear me? Now die . . . ."

Without waiting for blasts from the firing squad, Villa began emptying his own forty-five pistol. A frightened subordinate handed him another loaded pistol, and then another. Prisoners toppled to the ground. Blood soaked into the dirt. A raging Villa cursed and killed . . . .

The horrors of that blood-red dawn were in *Perro Negro's* eyes forever after. He witnessed that mass shooting. Later he had helped bury the bodies. When I met him, years ago, he pointed to the bullet-pocked 'dobe wall; he stood where the prisoners had been; he posed, mimicking Villa, his right arm extended as if holding a gun, and saying, "*Boom . . . Boom . . .*"

In atrocious Spanish he said, "Some of them pitched forward, *Señor*. Others leaped into the air, like frightened dogs. But they all died bravely. All but the man on the end. Ah, he was only a boy, and frightened. He turned to run, as a rabbit runs. Villa shot him before he reached the corner of the wall. Ah, what a sight, *Señor*. Would you like to see the body of the boy who ran?"

"His body is here?" I asked.

"Come, *Señor*," said Perro Negro proudly.

We walked past the bleak, sandy mounds of sagging wooden crosses, where occasional fruit jars contained flowers as dead and ugly as the cadavers beneath. Mid-way of the cemetery Perro Negro paused, then lifted an ancient, cellar-like door. A creaky ladder afforded us passage into the dingy, lime-splattered vault. In the darkness of the small, earthern tomb a crude coffin was visible. Beneath the glass lid lay a corpse.

Outside again the fresh air, I said, "What did you think of Villa, Perro Negro?"

Black Dog rolled his eyes. "Ah, what a man was Pancho! He did things, *Señor!*"

In the heat of battle, during the capture of Jimenez, Pancho and several of his Dorados came charging down a side street on lathered horses. A small girl, crying and clutching a tattered doll, stumbled and fell in her frantic effort to reach the sidewalk gate of a parochical school. A good Sister came running to the rescue, oblivious of the flying bullets.

Villa wheeled up, bellowing at his men, letting loose a blistering reprimand at the Sister. Then he caught a glimpse of the tearful urchin and saw the tell-tale pallor that comes from hunger. He leaped from his horse, clutched the girl up in his arms while tears filled his eyes.

"She is hungry, Sister?" he asked.

"Soldiers have confiscated most of the food in town," the Sister said humbly.

"You shall have food!" Villa promised.

A wagon load of food and supplies was delivered to the convent that night. As dictator of Chihuahua, Pancho saw to it that the state supplied all the schools with necessary funds for maintenance. He "adopted" several children through agents, sent them to the United States for their education, and paid the expenses out of his own pocket. To this day those "children" have no idea that their benefactor was Pancho Villa.

Louisa Villa was a favorite niece of Pancho's. When she was small he bounced her on his knee; he got down on the floor and amused her with his antics. He laughed when she laughed. He bought her a huge doll that said, "Mama."

Louisa grew up to be a beautiful girl. El Paso was her home.

"Uncle Pancho," she said quietly, "was one of the kindest men I've ever known. He loved children so very much."

7.

Star At The Zenith

T was bitterly cold that night of December 11, one of Villa's aides-de-camp related. "After moving through San Jesus Pass we could see the enemy campfires near the Camargo railroad station. The Federalistas were huddled around those fires trying to keep warm.

"The winter wind whipped out of the north, freezing us to the marrow. We tried running and jumping to keep from dying, but the exercise didn't help. Villa's orders were not to build any fires for fear the enemy would detect us. But by midnight the cold was so terrible we were afraid the horses would freeze to death.

"Villa came down the line of men then with orders to go ahead and build fires. My orderly and I soon had a fire going. We were behind a small hill. I took some of the hot ashes and made a bed. We were without blankets, so I wrapped myself in an old coat and laid down on the hot ashes. For a while I felt relief, but three hours later I awakened so stiff and cold I could hardly move. The coat I had been sleeping in was ashes.

"We were to attack at six o'clock. The minutes dragged. I kept looking at my watch. The soldiers were huddled together in groups. They were so cold their faces were blue. They kept asking what time it was. They wanted the battle to start so they could warm their hands on the hot barrels of their rifles.

"Villa kept walking up and down the line. Several times I heard him say, 'God, it's cold. God, it's cold.'

"At last the word came for the attack. The men came

to their feet and stumbled forward, heading for the station. General Uribe's men opened fire first. Villa instructed his Dorados to attack the home of General Rosalio Hernandez and bring him in dead or alive. We went there but found his home deserted.

"Villa then led us back to the station. We heard a lot of shooting, but it sounded like a one-sided battle. When we got to the scene of battle we saw what was happening then. The *Federalistas*, newly arrived from southern Mexico, were completely unaccustomed to the cold. They were actually frozen as stiff as statues. Their rifles were in their arms, but their trigger fingers were frozen.

"Our men advanced, shooting and yelling for them to drop their guns. Our men didn't understand at first. They wanted to get the battle over. The poor enemy devils cried out in pain and terror as they dropped to the ground.

"Nobody will ever know the horror of that sight except the men who were there. Everywhere I looked were corpses and blood on the ground. The nearby box-cars dripped blood. Some of the enemy escaped, but very few of them. General Uribe reported that General Hernandez had been in town, but had fled, leaving a considerable sum of money behind.

"General Uribe's talk stopped as a screaming, hysterical woman came running up to Villa. She dropped to her knees in front of him, sobbing, her arms outstretched.

" 'Please do not kill my husband! In your mother's name, please let him live!'

"Villa asked her who her husband was. She described him, saying that General Uribe had ordered some soldiers to take him away. Her husband, she said, was a civilian government employee. Then Villa turned to Uribe, asking him about the man.

"General Uribe replied, 'General, it is too late. He is already gone.'

"The woman, hearing the truth, rose to her feet. Never have I seen such hatred and loathing on a woman's face. She had the immense courage peculiar to our women. She beat Villa's chest with her fists. She spit on him. She shrieked, 'Assassin, thief! You murdering son of a bitch! Why don't you kill me . . . .?'

"I saw Villa's pistol leap into his hand. The shot almost tore off the woman's head. I looked away, sick to my stomach. Such crimes, I knew, were a necessary part of the revolution."

Mention should be made here of Villa's famed Dorados. They were organized in Ascension, Chihuahua, in 1913, and were called Villa's personal bodyguard. The group consisted of three squadrons of one hundred men in each squadron.

Each Dorado owned two horses. He was equipped with a 7mm carbine, a brace of .44 caliber Colt pistols, and 300 rounds of ammunition. He was an early day commando, a man chosen carefully for his iron nerve and courage.

In need of a quick victory, Villa sent in his "Golden Ones." If his ragtag *peon* soldiers began retreating, the Dorados turned the tide of battle. They were his shock troops, his pride and joy. He knew all of them by name. He purchased them 5-X Stetsons and olive drab uniforms. He had them drilled until they pranced with the precision of the White Horse Guard.

During one of his meetings with General Hugh L. Scott in Juarez, Villa insisted that the American general witness his Dorados perform on the parade grounds. After the Dorados had galloped past in rigid formation, Villa said:

"How do you like them, General?"

Said General Scott: "As a cavalry unit, General Villa, I assure you that I consider it the first in America."

"The men of Villa's staff," Manuel Gonzales said, "were as different in disposition, breeding and temperament as men could be."

One of Villa's "chosen few" was Felipe Angeles, one time president of Chalputepec, the military college. He had studied in France; he had the intelligent face and eyes of a devout scholar. As an artillery strategist, he was a genius, an authority, an author of text books. Small and rather delicately built, he was anything but a robust adventurer.

Upon Madero's assassination, General Felipe Angeles returned to Mexico. He had been a loyal believer in Madero. He believed in The Cause as religiously as a man believes in the Diety. His friendship for Villa was founded on understanding; their abiding devotion for each other was another paradox.

Rodolfo Fierro was another of Villa's intimates. If Villa was immoral, Fierro was doubly so. Fierro ostensibly set out to out-do the master. He won the name "The

Top: Villa soldiers on move through the mountains.
Middle: A troop train pulls out of Chihuahua City.
Below: Bodies of men killed by Villa in the Juarez cemetery.

Butcherer" — proudly so. His homicidal complex was as revolting to the civilized man as cannibalism.

Fierro simulated Villa's swagger. A one-time railroader, he excelled in the business of moving troops via the steel rails. For this reason alone Villa kept him on his staff. Fierro had beady black eyes, a heavy head of hair and a mustache. He was tall and powerfully built. Men feared him, hated him, distrusted him.

He killed men, he admitted, because he liked to watch death come into their eyes. He enjoyed the sight of blood. Not a drop of sentimentality or kindness was in him. It has been claimed that he killed at least one prisoner before breakfast each morning; then ate a huge meal. He drank heavily, but was never known to become intoxicated.

The quarrels between Villa and Fierro were many, and violent. Why Villa did not kill Fierro on various occasions still remains a mystery. Or why Fierro, with ambitions of his own, did not murder Villa is puzzling. Whatever the reasons, it remains a fact that Fierro, a murderous enigma, took Villa's tongue-lashings stoically; he remained at Villa's side, loyal to the end, like a great mastiff with a lust for blood.

General Borunda was another. He was a short man, of round, cherubic face and restless eyes. On occasion he was impetuous and gay; then again he was moody and sullen. Like Fierro, he had no more fear of death than of a spring shower. He killed and enjoyed it, but not with Fierro's gargantuan appetite.

Tomas Urbina was an original member of Villa's outlaw bunch. Fat-bellied and short, Urbina trailed along at Villa's coat-tail for one thing: gold! His love of money amounted to a mania. When banks or stores were looted, Urbina was there. He could neither write nor add figures, but he knew how to hoard money, this mustached, round-faced little man.

He walked with a chicken waddle, this Urbina. He professed a great love for Villa; and in return, Villa trusted him. He wept easily, but treachery and cunning were in him like a poison. Love of gold was his downfall. Villa, suddenly aware of Urbina's treachery, reluctantly killed the little fat man.

Villa displayed strange whims; his perspective was often out of focus. He distrusted men and women alike; but, strangely, the men he trusted most were the ones who rooked him. But that he dominated the lives of men like

Fierro, Borunda, Urbina and Angeles is a tribute to Villa's power.

With the capture of Juarez, Villa turned his army of four thousand men toward Chihuahua City. His star was at the zenith. He struck at Chihuahua, again employing tactics that caught the defenders off balance. He struck with all the ferocity of the ancient Aztecs. Like hunger-crazed wolves, his soldiers swarmed over the town. This was December 3, 1913.

Villa, now dictator of the State of Chihuahua, went into action with an energy and zest that inspired other men. He re-equipped his army with captured loot; he organized the White Cross, which was to care for the wounded; he relegated capable men to duties with the aplomb of a directing fire-chief. And the results were startling.

El Paso hailed the great Villa with a deluge of gilt-edged invitations, favors and a fanaticism that we great Americans perpetrate upon heroes. But Villa smiled and said no. Press men, feature writers and the fawning curious tagged after him. Bands played and people waved flags.

Villa kept himself isolated. Fierro got drunk.

Villa, the disciplinarian, cracked the whip and got action. He dislodged trembling officer-holders of uncertain political views and appointed men whom he knew he could trust. In Juarez, he cooperated with the American Custom Authorities to halt the dope traffic. From over the entire state he confiscated millions of dollars in currency and property, rebuilt public institutions and hospitals, increased the wages of school teachers, paved streets, built new railroads — and won the acclaim of the people.

He executed traitors, told the Church to continue with its Cause, but not to interfere with his. He broke up huge estates into small farms and gave the *peones* each a plot of land, as he had promised. He taxed the wealthy at gun-point and spent money as only Midas and Roosevelt have before or since.

General Carranza, strangling in the tide of Villa's popularity, edged on at a snail's pace toward Torreon. In Mexico City, Huerta continued to rant and fume.

Back in Juarez, Villa continued his lavish spending, tossing money around like confetti. From the Tri-State

Grocery Company he bought a carload of lard; Endicott, Johnson & Company got a lush order for 27,624 pairs of shoes; Jas. T. Leonard & Co., Inc., of New York got an order for 2,500 army hats — good ones. It was a buying spree that bolstered El Paso's business to a high water mark and excited certain money-grabbing merchants to the point of ulcers.

Hipolito Villa, Pancho's brother, acting as a purchasing agent, went to New York and headquartered at the Hotel Astor. His bank book on the Guaranty Trust Company of New York is one of my documentary souvenirs. The stub book shows expenditures that are reminiscent of the New Deal: Madero brothers were paid a total of $100,000; F. A. Sommerfield, holding an ammunition contract, was delivered checks amounting to $9275.60, $4081.00, $46,700.00, $40,000.00 and $80,000.00 — all within three weeks.

A full carload of gold and silver bullion arrived in Juarez and was immediately changed into American currency. From all indications there were several millions placed on deposit in New York banks, San Antonio and El Paso. Villa's purchasing agents had the plush carpets rolled out for them by the mercantile tycoons. The Winchester Firearms Company detailed a representative, an expense account unlimited, to remain at. Villa's beck and call.

Canned meats and foods were bought by the trainload. Clothing, shoes and war materiel rolled into Juarez in gigantic lots. Five airplanes were bought for the Villistas. American pilots were hired at exhorbitant salaries as instructors. Wooden train coaches were converted into armored cars and armed with machine guns. One coach, confiscated from a wealthy mining official, was refurbished in Old World elegance for Pancho's private car. Expensive automobiles were purchased for Villa, his brother Hipolito, and Pancho's staff.

"Buy only the best," ordered Villa. "And plenty of it."

Villa's fame now was front page stuff; it crowded news of the rising turmoil in Europe to page four. Red banner heads screamed of his eminence. Washington diplomats, despising Huerta, straddled the political fence but gave sly nods to Villa's agents, and waited like a group of uneasy Pontius Pilates. In spite of the sympathetic clamor, calliope-tooting and circus press agentry, Villa remained unchanged. He was too earthy to be swayed by the mob's applause. For a man who could neither read nor write his powers of perception were uncanny. Sham, prentense, hypocrisy — these things he hated with a passion.

"He was one sow's ear," said Bill Greet, "who refused to be made into a silk purse for society."

Stories and legends sprang up about Pancho that put dime fiction to shame. He was "colorful" and "different." Writers with kite-tail imaginations filled the newspapers and magazines with stories — some of them true, some wild flights of fantasy. The fact that Villa had been a bandit, a butcher, a philanderer made good reading.

There was news-value in everything he did or said. Exaggerations ran rampant about his loves, his generosity and sentimentality, his battle valor and quixotic moods. He was a man to watch. His killings were shocking, but good reading.

Villa often had his staff officers read to him of his various deeds. He chuckled. Such prominence seemed to vindicate his peon heritage. A few months later one of his agents paid an El Paso newspaper $10,000 each thirty days for "favorable" publicity.

Again, later in his campaign, Villa and his army were encamped west of Juarez, waiting to recapture the city. Norman Walker, a crack Associated Press man, got an interview with Villa ahead of the other newshawks. Pancho confided that his attack would start at dawn the next day. Walker smiled, long aware of Villa's front page propensity.

"Tomorrow is not a good day, General," he said.

Villa looked surprised. "Why?"

Walker explained. Tomorrow, he said, was the start of the World's Series ball games. *Americanos* loved base ball. The front pages would carry pictures of the players. The story of Villa's battle would, of necessity, drop back to the classified pages.

"Americans are strange people," said Pancho.

"They think the same of you, General Villa."

Pancho turned to his staff officers. "We shall hold off the attack, boys, until the Americans finish their ball game. We don't want those ball-playing birds to crowd us off the front pages."

The fact that Villa and his men *did* commit atrocities is undeniable. But has there ever been a war without atrocities? Many of the untidy deeds attributed to him are true; many are false. One has a choice of which to accept and which to deny.

One story, still current, is that Ambrose Bierce, a firebrand and man of letters, left the U. S. at the age of 72 and joined Villa for one last fling at adventure — and was brutally murdered by Villa for his trouble. When accused of the murder Villa made vehement denial. Admittedly, Pancho was no paragon of verity. Did he kill Ambrose Bierce? *Quien sabe?*

In the spring of 1914 a cutthroat renegade named Maximo Castillo took advantage of the turmoil and began plundering on his own. He and his *pelados* held up a Mexican train, stole the cash aboard, then headed the train into a burning tunnel. Fifty-one passengers and the crew were aboard. Three of the passengers were Americans. They all died.

It was a shocking atrocity to the civilized world. Fortunately for Villa, he was in Juarez at the time. He sent soldiers out for Castillo's hide, but the wary bandit escaped into the U. S. He was promptly imprisoned. This incident was known as the Cumbre Tunnel disaster.

Another incident, just as grisly, occured in April of 1916. Another Mexican train was heldup, its huge payroll taken. The 18 Americans aboard were cold-bloodedly murdered. The leader of the bandits was Pancho Lopez, a Villa officer. When captured, and just before his execution, he claimed that Villa had ordered him to commit the deed. This Villa denied just as vigorously. Was the ex-butcher really guilty?

William S. Benton was bull-dog British, hot-tempered when drinking, and very demanding. His ranch and mining properties were located near the town of Inde, Durango.

In February of 1914, he arrived in Juarez, full of demands, and about half full of bottled dynamite. Rustlers had been stealing his cattle. He wanted justice, instantly. It mattered not to him that Villa, up to his neck in personal troubles, was busy in a conference at headquarters.

Benton stormed past the outer guards to face Villa

Top: After the battle in Juarez 1914 - before the bodies of the dead men & horses were removed.
Below: Villa soldiers killed by American troopers during the retreat from Columbus.

at the latter's desk. The irate Englishman explained his mission; he wanted Villa to halt the rustling at his place, immediately. Villa ordered the man to make a quiet exit. Benton raged. Epithets bounced around the room like hail.

"Get out!" Villa roared.

Benton roared back. Then, it is claimed by witnesses, he made the horrible mistake of reaching for his pistol. Rodolfo Fierro, with his strong affinity for blood, was present. Who or how many shot first will never be known; but it is a fact that Mr. Benton's pistol was never discharged.

Villa's American supporters winced at the unfavorable publicity which followed. In London the British lion roared, started an investigation, and demanded that Villa be extradited for trial by English courts. Benton was buried — no one to this day knows where.

When asked of the occurrence, Villa shrugged and said, "Benton reached for his gun first. He was a plain damn fool."

8.

The Falling Star

HAT cold March morning of March 4, 1914, ten full train loads of soldiers and materiel of war pulled out of the Juarez station. The populace lined the tracks, waving flags, yelling themselves hoarse, their voices rising above the martial band music. Villa sat at a window in his private coach, smiling. His boots were on the floor nearby; his feet hurt. Across from him sat Fierro and Urbina.

"Torreon first," said Villa. "Then Mexico City."

Said the *El Paso Times:* "General Francisco Villa was welcomed back to the city of Chihuahua with unbounded enthusiasm. Half of the population was at the station to meet him."

In Chihuahua City, already a Villa stronghold, the train halted only long enough for more trains to join the mighty parade. Thousands of soldiers, burdened with gear, piled on top the freight cars. Some of the men had their women with them; these were the *soldaderas*, the peon-soldier's commissariat — tragic-eyed women, squaws of the revolution, who followed their menfolk with bovine loyalty.

Somewhere up the line, two small villages made a token display of resistance. Those villagers might as well have tried to halt the floor waters of an arroyo by waving flags. The mighty tide rolled on: men swaying atop the freight cars, some singing *La Cucaracha*, the Villa war song, the women clinging to ludicrous belongings.

More than fifty thousand men! Villa's men! Artillery in command of General Angeles. The Dorados, lusting for battle, anxious to prove their mettle. Horses and gear. Shrill-voiced *soldaderas*. *Peones* in ragged jeans and frayed *huaraches*, following the Pied Piper, clutching antiquated rifles.

March 19, 1914, they had Torreon surrounded. Outlying suburbs fell, but the main part of the city fought stubbornly. A cry rose, *Send in the Dorados!* The Golden Ones went in, like a mighty tornado of destruction. No living force could have stopped them. But it took fourteen bloody days of fighting to make victory complete. An estimated seven thousand men — and women — died. It was the bloodiest battle of the entire revolution. The wounded alone numbered thousands.

General Velasco, the Federal commander, with his shattered army remnants, retreated southward to the city of Zacatecas.

In Mexico City, Huerta raved like a maniac. He ordered the gunboat Zaragoza to stand by at Vera Cruz, ready for instant sailing. He had it loaded with provisions. The *El Paso Times* said: "Sentries guard the approaches to the ship and rumors persist that she intends to take aboard President Huerta or some other high official. It is also rumored that she carried a large consignment of gold."

Times headlines screamed: HUERTA'S END NOT FAR AWAY: HUERTA'S FRIENDS FEAR HIS REASON IS GIVING AWAY.

The noose was tightening. Huerta tried desperately to find soldiers to send to General Velasco's assistance, but his troops were deserting. Carranza also was making revolutionary inroads. To add to the confusion, a group of U. S. Marines got leave of their ship in Tampico harbor and went shore to see the sights. Huerta's officials, angered at Washington's non-recognition policy, promptly arrested the leather-necks.

Washington, thoroughly aroused, called it an international incident. They demanded release of the marines immediately. Mexican authorities acquiesced to the demand and said they were sorry. But the trouble was done; the water was boiling.

Then at Vera Cruz, trouble popped again, only louder. A ship from Germany was unloading huge quantities of ammunition. American cruisers in the harbor stood ready. Washington demanded more than just "sorry" talk from Mexico over the previous incident. Mexican officials sulked. Washington demanded action, and got it.

U. S. Marines unloaded, took possession of the ammunition-loaded ship *and* Vera Cruz. Shooting was inevitable. Several Mexican cadets and a few soldiers were killed. Rioting against Americans broke out in Mexico City. Inflamed Americans north of the border said war was at hand. Villa watched the anti-American sentiment flare, but remained silent.

General Carranza, on the other hand, made his bid for recognition. He contacted the head of the American forces in command of Vera Cruz. He represented himself as "First Chief of the Constitutionalist Army." He talked eloquently. *And the U. S. Government promised its support!* The American troops were immediately withdrawn.

In the governmental palace, Huerta stood staring like a stricken man, peering down upon the city. He had seen Diaz fall by a military *coup;* all too vividly he remembered the night Madero and Suarez were assassinated. The old Indian was done; his shoulders sagged.

The night of July 16, he fled, deafening himself to the cataclysmic upheaval behind him. A ship at Vera Cruz carried him to Cuba, then Europe. At the same time Pascual Orozco, a Huerta ally, vanished from the Mexican scene.

Exactly one year later, in July of 1915, an El Paso-bound train was halted at Newman, a water stop twenty miles northeast of El Paso. Federal men stepped aboard. They moved among the passengers until they found the two men they sought. Those two men were Victoriano Huerta and Pascual Orozco.

"We want you, gentlemen," said one of the U. S. Government men, "for conspiring against the neutrality laws existing between the United States and Mexico."

Both men were jailed. Later they were released, after raising huge cash bonds. Orozco fled. He was killed September 2 — along with five cohorts — in Green River Canyon, near Sierra Blanca, Texas. Orozco and his men had stolen horses from the Bob Love ranch and were on their way to Hot Springs, Texas, to meet with other revolutionary sympathizers. They were killed by members of the 13th Cavalry, custom officials and a posse of cowboys.

Huerta broken and sick, was allowed to live with his family in El Paso. He accepted his fate with the same stoical calmness he had displayed earlier in his career. Death and tragedy were not new to him. Toward the end, he embraced religion and asked for the last rites of the Catholic church.

He died quietly, expressing a love for Mexico with his last words.

Upon Huerta's abdication, a *pro tem* president appeared by the name of Eulalio Gutierrez. Villa nodded his head with satisfaction; but Carranza, still stinging from the lash of Villa's insults, violently disagreed as to Gutierrez' office-holding, and persuaded Obregon to join him. This Carranza-Obregon alliance was to eventually cause Villa's downfall.

In November of 1914, Villa gave the greatest performance of his career. He and his famed Dorados rolled into Mexico City on a special train. The entire populace turned out in one of the most stupendous celebrations the city had ever witnessed. Flags waved and people cheered, bands played and the roar of the crowd was heard miles away.

As the automobile carrying Villa and the president of Mexico edged through the throng, it was Villa's name that echoed to the heavens — not the president's. Pancho, the bandit and ex-butcher, had all of Mexico in the palm of his hand. He was a fighter, this Villa — a gambler with Life. All of Mexico was at his feet, screaming, weeping for sheer joy.

Villa smiled and waved; he glanced back at his marching Dorados and gained reassurance. In that moment his star shone its brightest.

In the days that followed, Villa visited with the new president almost daily. They discussed affairs of the government; and Villa displayed an astute knowledge of civil operations that surprised even the most learned. He posed in the president's chair for a picture. In a secret caucus he was offered the presidency, but he turned it down.

"I am not qualified to be president," he said. "I am a fighter, and there is still fighting to be done."

When word reached the capital that the Carranza-Obregon forces were growing in strength, Villa hurried back to Juarez, there to buy more war supplies. Rumor had it that Woodrow Wilson, the new U. S. president, was on the verge of accepting Villa as the Mexican government *in toto*. Such recognition was what Villa had been hoping for.

By April of 1915, Villa had his army well-equipped and was on the march again. Word reached him that Carranza had control of Mexico City; that General Obregon was in Celaya. Confident of victory, Villa asked his favorite general, Tomas Urbina, to join him with the Urbina troops. Why Urbina ignored this Villa order has never been determined. But ignore it he did.

Against the advice of General Angeles, Villa attacked Obregon at Celaya — and suffered a Bull Run defeat, the first of many to follow. He retreated to Torreon, then Chihuahua City. His star had dimmed. It has been said that no one can fall faster than a man who has enjoyed a perch on the top rung of a ladder.

Such was the case now with Villa. Defeat followed defeat. He shook himself like a huge mastiff who has been mauled by a little Fido. Then like a bolt from the blue came a flash over the wires — that memorable day of October 12, 1915:

PRESIDENT WILSON FORMALLY APPROVES PAN AMERICAN PLAN TO ACCORD RECOGNITION TO CARRANZISTAS.

Villa at first was stunned. Then he broke loose in a tantrum so violent no man dared to talk to him. He cursed and raged; he threatened death to every American he could lay a hand on; he called President Wilson all the hide-blistering epithets in the Mexican language.

Then, October 14 — two days later — came another jolt, as shocking as the first. The *El Paso Times* broke with the following headlines and story:

THE EMBARGO OF ARMS TO MEXICO IS ON!

"The embargo on munitions became effective this morning, when military authorities held up a shipment of twenty cases of cannon powder which was presented for export to the Villa faction in Juarez. The powder will be held by military authorities. It was further announced from military headquarters that any attempt to export munitions to the Villa faction would be stopped by the military."

The Winchester Arms representative made a swift exit; his job was done. It was up to smugglers and gun-runners to keep Villa supplied with war essentials now. General Hugh L. Scott, termed the American peace-maker, criticized President Wilson hotly, saying, "He went against all his promises!"

In Juarez, Villista General Tomas Ornelas traitorously surrendered the town and garrison to the Carranza government without firing a shot.

To facilitate quick movement, and to gain a military *coup*, the United States permitted Carranza's troops to travel by train from El Paso to Douglas, Arizona. Result: Villa's troops suffered another defeat in Sonora.

Shall we call this American intervention?

Villa staggered under the smashing blows like a boxer dazed and hurt, knowing he was done, and knowing that some of the blows were below the belt line. In white-faced, helpless fury he watched his men desert. With only a few followers behind him, he found refuge in the hills. Word came that the very people who, just a year before, had blessed him as a hero were now calling him a bandit.

General Obregon and Carranza were the country's idols. Villa, they said, like water, had found his level. They placed a 100,000 peso reward for his capture dead or alive.

Villa licked his sores. The new scars, like the ones on his back, would remain over his heart. He swore that he was not done; that the entire world would hear of his "comeback." But before he made *big* plans he had a job to do — several of them. Again we find him ruled by his elemental instincts and emotions. Once more the desire for revenge was like a roaring inferno inside him.

General Tomas Urbina had double-crossed him at the battle of Celaya. Also Villa knew that Urbina had absconded with a fortune in cash and jewels from the Villista coffers.

Villa and a handful of his men made a lengthy ride to

Urbina's Chihuahua *rancho*. The unsuspecting Urbina was caught just as he was in the act of departing for Texas — with dreams of luxurious living the rest of his days.

Villa turned to Fierro, the butcherer. "You'll have to do it, *compañero*," Pancho said. "I have known Urbina too long . . . ."

Fierro emptied his pistol. The fat Urbina, his belly torn with lead, dropped to the ground, dead.

General Tomas Ornelas, the traitorous Juarez commander, was next. He died while on his knees pleading for mercy. Villa did this "job" without Fierro's assistance.

Then Villa returned to Sonora, riding by night for safety's sake. He began recruiting a new army, but the *peones*, weary of war and bloodshed, were slow in responding. While on another mission, Rodolfo Fierro drowned. It is claimed that Villa wept like a child.

Weeks passed. One night in the mountainous region of Chihuahua, Villa called his men together. All the old fire was back in Villa's eyes; he had pieced together the old dreams — shoddily, perhaps, but still dreams of power and grandeur. And revenge.

"Villa is not through!" he exhorted. "Wait and see . . . ."

And some of his loyal followers believed him.

9.

The Columbus Raid

I N the spring of 1916, Columbus, New Mexico drowsed in the desert silence, peaceful and calm; and when the sun became too warm the loafers in front of Dean's Grocery Store moved their chairs.

A lone Mexican trudged along the dusty, sun-baked street. Behind him trailed a sleepy burro with great bundles of mesquite roots loading him down. Hunkered down beside the loafers a pink-cheeked youth in the uniform of a U. S. Army private grinned and said:

"You don't see sights like that back in Chicago."

One of the men, a tall, booted and big-hatted rancher,

Top: American soldiers digging graves on the outskirts of Columbus the day following the raid.

Below: American soldiers standing beside the coffins of their comrades who were killed during the Columbus raid.

said, without turning, "There's a heap of things you'll see down here that you don't see in Chicago, son. One of the things is trouble — in big hunks."

The soldier laughed. "If you mean Villa trouble, you're wrong, mister. He'd never have the nerve to come this close to the border. Anyhow, he's done."

They fell silent as the noon-day train from El Paso rumbled up to a halt, hissing steam and panting, in front of the yellow-frame El Paso & Southwestern railroad station. Jess Fuller came out of the grocery and walked the hundred yards to the station. After the train pulled out, Fuller returned to where the loafers were sitting. His face was grave as he scanned a newspaper headline.

'Read this," he said to one of the men. "It's this morning *El Paso Times.*"

The newspaper was dated March 8, 1916. The headlines and lead story said:

VILLA EXPECTED TO ATTACK PALOMAS

Information received in El Paso last night from the 13th cavalry, stationed at Columbus, New Mexico, was to the effect that Villa had been sighted 15 miles west of Palomas Monday night and was camped there all day Tuesday. What his plans are at this time are not known.

Villa is reported to have between 300 and 400 men with him. They are all well mounted and since arriving near Palomas have been slaughter-large numbers of cattle.

There is but a small Carranza garrison at Palomas and it is believed that Villa intends making an attack on the town.

Those men read the story with varying opinions; they knew Villa was fighting with the desperation of a cornered puma. But with 120 regular soldiers of the 13th cavalry stationed there in town they felt little concern for their own safety. Colonel Slocum, the commanding officer, had for weeks assured the little town of 300 population that there was no cause for alarm.

And for weeks the inhabitants of Columbus had watched the soldiers drill. They were almighty proud of the town and the way it was growing. The soldiers spent their pay; the merchants thrived. Broadway, the main street, ran east and west; it boasted of a hardware store operated by J. L. Walker, J. T. Dean's grocery, C. Dewitt Miller's drug store, the Hoover Hotel and a score of smaller businesses.

Most prententious of the stores was the Ravel Brothers Mercantile, on Boulevard Street. Sam and Louis Ravel were known for miles around as stolid merchants with eyes for business. They handled bolt goods and cooking utensils for the housewives ;boots, overalls for the men, and all the sundry articles a frontier folk would want.

They lived in the rear of the store. When Arthur, their twelve year old brother, came to live with them he was immediately put to work as chore boy. They enjoyed a patronage from across the line, and went out of their way to encourage Mexican trade. The Mexicans paid cash. If they wanted guns and ammunion, who would have the affront to question their use for such fire-arms?

The Ravel brothers were not inquisitive by nature. They could out-shrug a Mexican. Did the Ravels enjoy lush profits by selling the Villistas huge quantities of guns and ammunition? And was there a shortage of $2500 worth of war supplies to Villa — paid for in advance — which prompted Villa to make the Columbus raid to "square the account?"

On Taft Street, near the railroad station, was the two-story frame Commercial Hotel, operated by Mr. and Mrs. W. T. Ritchie. Across from it was a movie theater. Opposite the railroad tracks, south of town, was the army encampment.

One has the feeling of vast expanse in Columbus. Exactly thirty-two miles north, straddling Highway 80, is the prosperous town of Deming. South of Columbus three miles is the boundary line. When you cross the railroad track in Columbus, the American Customs men halt you. Big, tall, level-eyed Jack Breen is there at the Customs station. He remembers the Villa raid well: Jack Breen was there when it happened.

Jack has a slow smile and the respect of everyone who knows him. "Things might have been different in Columbus," he says," — if it hadn't been for the raid."

Back of the Customs house is Villa Hill. a landmark of dark lava stone and scant brush. Directly in front of the Customs station is a huge arroyo — a natural ditch which runs parallel to the road the full three miles to the border.

A high wire fence marks the border, running east and

west for several miles. Here are the Mexican Customs; here is Palomas: treeless, sunbaked and somnolent — a quaint village of squat 'dobe buildings, surrounded by the limitless brush, quiet, serene. When the mission bell tolls you start. A rider jogs past the *cantinas;* a mongrel rises from the dust to scratch itself. Two men in huge sombreros stand in the shade of a doorway; they speak courteously as you pass. From out of the hush comes the tinkle of a guitar, a gentle voice in song.

"Like Columbus," you say, "nothing much could ever happen here."

But something did.

Juan Favela, foreman for the extensive Palomas Land and Cattle Company, was riding through the high mesquite five miles south of the border the afternoon of March 8, 1916. The Palomas Land and Cattle Company was American owned, although the vast, king-size estate was in Mexico. Since early morning Juan and some *vaqueros* had been rounding up stray cattle.

It was rough, wild country. Juan left his men and turned his horse toward the headquarters ranch, several miles to the west. Juan was a realist, not given to illusions. He was a capable man, highly respected for his integrity.

Suddenly, as he topped a hill, he caught a glimpse of a large force of riders below him. One glance was enough for him to identify the army of horse-backers. He whirled his horse, heading for Palomas. As he shot through the customs gate he yelled to the Mexican officers. They recognized him and divined the import of his Paul Revere haste.

On a lathered horse he covered the three miles to the army encampment in Columbus in record time. He excitedly demanded an audience with Colonel Slocum. The stern army colonel listened as Juan revealed his findings. Pancho Villa, said Juan, had at least five hundred men with him; they were heading for the border; they were just south of Palomas; they would raid Columbus before dawn!

Colonel Slocum, a disciple steeped in the sanctity of border-lines and covenants, listened to the report calmly. He suggested that Juan go have a drink; then taper off. Juan pleaded his case. Colonel Slocum was definitely not interested.

"Colonel Slocum should have listened to Juan Favela," Jess Fuller said later. "Why he and some of the other officers left Columbus that night is a mystery. Lieutenant Castleman was officer of the day. He more or less took charge of things when the shooting started."

That night the darkness seemed filled with eerie whisperings. Stars glimmered in the heavens. The heat of the day subsided as a cool, gentle breeze sprang up. The pungent desert air was filled with the unforgettable fragrance of greasewood.

The scattered buildings of Columbus were dark for the most part. Kerosene lamps inside the railroad station burned dismally; a weary dispatcher sat at his desk. Two windows in the Commercial Hotel were yellow with light. At a desk in his room a cigar drummer worked late over his report. Beyond the center of town the 'dobe homes stood like inverted boxes in the darkness — huddled together as if for protection.

South of the track the army camp was a sea of dark tents. A sentry stopped his pacing, listening. An alien sound touched his ears. Imagining things, he told himself, and went on. But some ominous, intangible threat persisted. Ghostly sounds ebbed and flowed; man-made sounds of furtive movements. Then the throbbing silence of the desert.

Three miles away, Villa and 600 hundred of his men circled Palomas. They were heavily armed with rifles, pistols and bandoleers. Thonged to some of the saddles were 5-gallon cans of kerosene.

One mile west of Palomas they cut a hole in the high wire fence. The riders crossed into the United States. Slowly, cautiously, they moved eastward toward the big ditch. A signal passed down the line of riders for a halt. As they waited, three men merged out of the darkness. They held a brief consultation with Villa.

It is known now that these three Villistas, experts with knives, crawled up to an American army outpost and killed the two soldiers on duty there. Captain "Bull" Studgy's outpost, a quarter mile farther east, was by-passed

When they reached the ditch, Villa strung his men out in a long line. They started northward, toward Columbus, moving with Indian stealth. The muffled click of a horse's hoof and the creak of leather were the only sounds. The darkness was in their favor. And the deep ditch which hid their movements.

It took them a long time to reach Columbus. The town was completely enveloped in darkness. Peering over the ditch bank, those Villistas got their bearings. The station loomed up before them. A hundred yards away was the army camp; they saw the sentry, limned against the stars, slowly pacing his beat.

The Villistas turned to watch their leader. He was only a dark shadow. But they saw his arm raise. It was the signal.

The thunderous blare of the Villistas' rifles split wide the night, echoing over the sleeping town like the deafening voice of doom. The sentry dropped. Then on a wave of killing passion, Villa and his men clamored out of the ditch, some afoot and some mounted. Across the town they swarmed, shooting and yelling, smashing windows and door-fronts. They fired at every moving shadow; they looted stores, burning and killing and destroying.

In the red flare of burning buildings, it was a tableau of death and horror, a reenactment of Dante's Inferno. Americans, half dressed and dazed, fought valiantly to protect their homes. They barricaded their doors and emptied their rifles. Screams of the women and children were all but lost in the din.

Dean's grocery store went up in flames. While it was still burning, Dean left his home and made a wild dash toward the store. He staggered and fell, riddled with bullets, before he had gone fifty feet. The Commercial Hotel was a roaring holocaust; Mrs. Ritchie managed to escape, but her husband was killed. Some other guests in the hotel were caught like rats in a trap.

Miller, the druggist, died trying to protect his store. Dr. H. M. Hart, W. A. Davidson, J. J. Moore and N. R. Walker were among the first to die.

At the army camp Lieutenant Castleman and his men were trying frantically to break into the guard-house. And what a strange commentary on army procedure: *The guard-house was locked with the rifles and ammunition inside!*

With what arms they could find unlocked, Castleman and his troopers opened fire. They found a machine-gun. After one splendid burst, it jammed. Major Tompkins and some other troopers showed up. They spread out, crept toward town — and made every shot count.

Ravel's Mercantile store claimed the attention of most of the raiders. They smashed the windows, broke down the doors. High above the bedlam rose the cry, mixed with profanity: *"Where is Sam Ravel?"* Inside the store they searched every nook and crevice, stealing and destroying as they went.

"Sam Ravel," explained Jess Fuller, "was in El Paso that night. He had gone there for some dental work. Louis Ravel was in the store alone. When the raiders struck, Louis hid under some cowhides at the rear of the store. Those Villistas began tearing the pile of cowhides apart. When they got down to the last few hides they quit. Luck sure rode with Louis that night. He was flattened out beneath that last hide.

"Some of Villa's men caught young Arthur Ravel farther down the street. The kid was in his underwear. Two Villista officers started back to the store with him. In the light of the burning buildings, Lieutenant Castleman saw them and killed both of the Villa officers. Young Arthur broke loose and ran four miles before he stopped for breath."

For two hours the battle raged. Then as dawn broke the Villa bugler blew retreat. On horses and afoot they raced toward the fence gate at Palomas. By this time the soldiers and civilians had gathered their wits and were organized. In the running fight which followed more than sixty of the raiders were killed.

Major Frank Tompkins, with approximately 50 American troopers, continued the chase into Mexico. Villa threw back a rear guard to halt the pursuit. A brief battle ensued. Then the outnumbered Americans returned to Columbus for re-inforcements.

The *El Paso Times*, dated March 10, devoted the entire front page to the raid. One story reads as follows:

"After the American troops had followed Villa for about 18 miles the bandits threw out a strong rear guard, which met the advancing cavalry and a sharp fight followed. The chase was then abandoned by the American troopers.

The attack on Columbus was wholly unsuspected, and Villa was in the town before any one knew of his presence. His soldiers cried "Viva Villa," and

"Death to the gringos!" They shot every American civilian who was on the street and then shot through the windows and doors of the residences.

Villa was in the center of his men urging them on. He told them to give the Americans no quarter and to kill men, women and children. He was identified by many residents of the town. Villa was attired in his military uniform and waved a sword.

When his men started retreating he flew into a frenzy and stabbed and slashed at those near him, telling them to continue fighting. But they retreated and when the line was reached, Villa was leading.

"17 Americans, eight soldiers and nine civilians, including a woman, are dead as a result of the attack. In the fight that followed the bandits were driven across the line, leaving fully 125 dead on the field of battle.

List of the dead:

Dr. H. M. Hart
W. A. Davidson
W. T. Ritchie
J. T. Dean
C. Dewitt Miller
J. J. Moore
N. R. Walker
An unidentified hotel guest
Sgt. John Nievergelt, band
Corporal Paul Simon, band
Corporal Harry Wiswell, Troop G
Private James Butler, Troop K
Frank T. Kindvall, Troop K
Private Fred Griffin, Troop K
Corporal Michael Barmazel, M. G. T.
Private Jesse P. Taylor, Troop F
Private James Venner, Troop M
Private John C. Yarborough, Troop K
Private Theodore Katzorke, Troop K
Lieutenant C. C. Benson
Captain G. Williams

Top: Bodies of dead raiders were tossed into pile, soaked with gasoline and burned.

Below: Terrified men and women, civilians of Columbus, fleeing from the stricken town after the shooting stopped.

Otis Aultman, Associated Press photographer, was the first camera man to arrive on the scene after the raid. He drove the seventy-five miles from El Paso in record-breaking time. The town was in smoldering ruins, the people still hysterical.

"Major Tompkins and his men returned while I was there. The major let loose some cussing that turned the air blue. He begged Colonel Slocum — who had put in his appearance — for more men to pursue Villa, but was refused.

That memorable day of March 9, 1916, Columbus, New Mexico rocketed to fame. In a matter of hours the State National Guard was on the scene. Other soldiers unloaded from Fort Bliss. Telegraph wires hummed. The hue and cry was: "Get Villa! Kill the murderous —!"

The dead Mexicans were hauled to a spot one mile east of town, soaked with gasoline and burned. The terrible stench of that human pyre remained in the air for months, according to Jess Fuller. It was estimated that between 175 and 200 bodies were in that grisly pile, not including the dead horses. The eighteen Villista prisoners were taken to Deming. Nine of them were subsequently hanged and the other nine were hurried off to the prison in Santa Fe.

In Washington war talk swelled to strident proportions. Prompt, decisive action was demanded. Whatever the cost, Villa had to be punished for his Columbus atrocity. Carranza protested when informed by President Wilson that polite dallying was at an end, and that American troops would go into Mexico for Villa's hide.

Carranza troops could, if they so desired, render assistance to the American soldiers in their chase. If, said Wilson, they did not care to cooperate, it made no difference. The U. S. was tired of insults and abuse.

March 15, 1916, General John J. Pershing with ten thousand American troops crossed the line into Mexico. In some of the Mexican villages the U. S. troops were received cordially; the Mexicans liked the feel of the American dollar after the worthless Villa currency. In other Mexican towns the temper of the natives was explosive; they resented the troopers' presence and displayed their resentment by throwing rocks, mud, offal, and firing a few shots.

In Carrizal, Mexican troops under General Felix Gomez, ordered the Americans to halt. The Americans went on. A battle ensued in which the outnumbered Americans paid the costly price of 17 killed, many wounded and several captured.

On February 7, 1917 — with the war in Europe beckoning — General Pershing led his men out of Mexico. The abortive one year chase after Villa had failed miserably; it had gained nothing but ill feeling, blistered feet, and a definite taste among some of the "boys" for Carta Blanca beer.

Jess Fuller was mayor of Columbus, New Mexico for twelve years. He had been a lawman, a jailer in Deming, a barber, a pool hall operator, and a restauranteur. He was in Columbus the night of the raid, living in a shack near the Commercial Hotel.

"The raid." said Jess, "started at exactly 4:20 in the morning and lasted until 6:20 — two hours. Villa's men were mostly farmers, but I'll never forget the hophead in the crowd. He was a bad one, that hophead.

"When all the hell started to pop I rolled a big barrel up in front of my shack door and got behind it. Sure, I got in a few good shots. Funny setup, that raid. I'll never sabe why Colonel Slocum didn't listen to Juan Favela. But the one thing I'll never be able to explain is why I didn't shoot Villa's bugler. He wasn't over fifty feet away, and mounted on a grey horse when he blew for retreat. I could have shot him easy enough. But I just sat there, watching. Funny."

'Sus Carreon operates the U. S. Market in Columbus today. He has a nice smile, a sparkling wit and the respect of all who know him. "My Dad and I were a few miles below the line the afternoon before the raid," said 'Sus. "We had some mules down there, and knowing that Villa was in the vicinity, we thought we would herd them to the U. S. side. I was only a kid then, but I did the work of two men, whipping those mules north.

"We felt sure that, on this side of the line, the mules would be safe. Well sir, we hadn't any more than crossed over when Villa struck. He didn't get us, but he got the mules. Boy, that hurt, him getting those mules. If we had left them where they were down in Mexico they'd have been safe."

One can safely say that no other event in American history has caused more arguments than the Villa raid on Columbus. Get six people together and you will likely get six different versions. Little wonder is it then that some writers, after spending a day in Columbus gathering cursory interviews, return to their typewriters and let fly with their own hair-raising version.

Nor, in view of the facts, is it surprising that some historians let loose with poisonous barbs and vitriolic editorial comment which makes good reading, but tends to obscure the actual happenings.

To record the rumors, the bitter accusations, and the "factual" testimonies relative to the raid would, in itself, comprise a volume of interesting composition. With much vehemence it has been argued that Villa was not in Columbus during the raid. With sly nods, and please-don't-quote-me-but it's a fact whisperings, the tale still persists that President Wilson and his Cabinet *hired* Villa to make the raid so as to arouse the American people to a state of warmindedness.

Unfounded rumors are still to be heard that Villa was paid an enormous sum of money to perpetrate the raid, that he could have been captured subsequent to the raid many times — but orders from "higher up" said let him go.

Ugly gossip sometimes tells, with dark implications, that the whole thing was a frame-up; that the American army officers were unaccountably thirty miles from Columbus that night, drinking; that because of earth-shaking testimony later produced by an investigating committee at Fort Bliss, the investigation was squashed.

To give credence to such flamboyant tongue-wagging is like listening to the lyre-plucking of Orpheus as he flits from one poppy to another.

That Villa led the Columbus raid is a matter of record, written in blood. Why some people hesitate to accept this fact is puzzling. Villa, with his monumental ego, was never one to stand coyly in the shadows and let other men do the job at hand.

A friend of mine, now a highly esteemed business man in San Antonio, was one of Villa's colonels. For numerous reasons I shall call him Tony Garcia. That is not his real name, but it will suffice.

Tony Garcia was with the Villistas during the raid on Columbus. The past is dead for him; he is trying to forget it. I trust his word implicitly.

"Villa led the raid on Columbus," said Tony Garcia. *Señora* Luz Corral recently said, "On March 9, 1916, Pancho Villa, *in person* with some of his men, entered, at dawn, the small American town of Columbus . . . ."

Villa was an exhibitionist with a goal; he was a frustrated *peon* with the fighting and revengeful instincts of Neanderthalian man. He made the Columbus raid to sate his desire for vengeance. He hated President Wilson, claiming he, Villa, had been double-crossed; he hated Americans generally, particularly those who took his money and sold him short.

The Columbus raid was testimony of Villa's wrath; it was his last frenzied, desperate gunblast of retaliation.

Columbus might have been the center of a thriving, irrigated farming community if Fate had dealt the cards differently. Overnight it roared into fame. Townspeople fled, and new people came in; but the people who flocked there were not town builders: they were the curious, the gamblers, the parasitical camp followers.

After the bubble burst the natives remained; they and their children are there today. They have their dreams and their memories. But they are looking ahead, planning, building solidly on the bedrock of faith. Their courage is magnificent; their quiet hospitality is an aura of godliness.

Like ugly monuments over the scattered town are bullet-pocked ruins, ancient foundations and decaying land-marks—mute evidences of devastation. But the 365 people in Columbus today look beyond the ruins and point to their churches and school, their new homes; they tell of their healthful climate and the opportunities. A town like that can never die.

Jess Fuller owns the Onyx Cafe in Columbus. He is never rushed with patronage; he wouldn't want it that way.

He'd rather sit out in front and be "neighborly."

Across town Floyd Blair lives alone in a comfortable little home. Floyd is 64, and blind. This gentle, white-haired oldtimer was a realtor years ago. He has time-yellowed maps of Columbus showing the streets and building plots — and non-existent sub-divisions. His dreams, too, were wrecked; but he smiles and says, "Columbus will come back."

Today the people of Columbus and Palomas are as one; they visit and inter-marry, enjoying a friendship based upon understanding. And whether you are in Pete Avillar's place in Palomas, or in Columbus, you're likely to hear someone say, not with historical accuracy, but pride:

"First time a foreign army ever invaded the Continental United States was right here."

10.

The Curtain Falls

HERE were more battles to be fought by Villa against the Carranzistas which, if catagorically listed, would be more repetitious than interesting. Time after time he hurled his men into conflict with fanatical ragings; he won towns and lost them. His temper was explosive, dangerous; his bitter cries, once so enthralling, fell upon the deaf ears of a Mexican people who were weary of bloodshed.

"Very few of us are left," he shouted at his soldiers. "But do not lose courage. I promise you and my people that I will always be your chief. I feel strong enough to fight Carranza forty more years."

Yet he was done, his race run. There was no martial music now, no frenzied cries of approval from the populace, no flag-waving and heroic shouts. No longer did men leave their families and come running to his Cause.

Again he sought the safety of the mountains, hounded and hunted by his own government and U. S. troops. Once he was accidentally wounded, and for ten days he and two of his men hid in — what he termed — Coscomate Cave. They subsisted on a scant three pounds of rice and the muddy water in their canteens. Sick and emaciated, they

Top: American soldiers cross into Mexico after Villa.

Below: U. S. supply wagons ford the shallow Rio Grande River in their quest for Villa.

peered into the heat-drenched valley below them and watched American soldiers dig up the horse that Villa had ridden to death.

"The fools!" Villa cried out fiercely. "The stupid fools!"

Meantime, in Mexico City, General Obregon was playing Mexican political poker with two aces up his sleeve and a loaded pistol in his pocket. At the table with him, two allies watched the game, waiting for the pot to be split. They were General Plutarco Elias Calles and Adolfo de la Huerta. Across from them sat Carranza, the victim.

The end for Carranza was an act so tiresomely old to the Mexican populace that they left the theater in disgust. May 21, 1920, Carranza tried to flee from assassins, but was murdered by the men guarding him.

Now with Villa's days numbered, Calles and Obregon shoved Adolfo de la Huerta into the president's hot seat. When news of this unsavory wool-gathering reached Villa, he was ready to quit. All his dreams, hopes and plans came crashing down to earth around him. The flaming hate inside him subsided to a smoldering bed of ashes; his power was gone. No living man, he knew now, could ever rule the destiny of Mexico.

Villa resigned himself to fate. Like a wayward husband finding his philandering suddenly tiresome, he longed for Luz Corral's welcoming smile. When friends went to his assistance and procured a grant of amnesty from the Mexican government, Villa was profoundly moved.

The terms of the government proffer were so graciously bountiful as to simulate Yuletide gifts. Where Villa's usual wariness was at the time no one can know. He took the offer hook, line, sinker and pole. The stipulated agreement was that Canutillo Rancho, State of Durango, was to belong to Villa — the entire 500,000 acres. The government would supply money for all equipment needs, farming tools and building repairs. Villa's men, like himself, were to receive a lush pension; they would not be molested by any political factions in power or out; each man was to be alloted his own farm.

Villa talked by telephone to President de la Huerta. The beatific *presidente* confirmed the terms of the contract, asking only that Villa refrain henceforth from any political harrangues, or shooting. Villa agreed.

Villa returned to Luz Corral's arms, forgetting his other wives with enchanting innocence. At Canutillo

Top: Some of the 'dobe ruins still standing in Columbus today, symbolical of the violence and bloodshed of another era, with fairly new white church in background. Lower: Columbus, New Mexico today is tranquil and prosperous, proud of its heritage, site of Pancho Villa State Park - attracting tourists and new residents, and hometown of Bill McGaw "The Southwesterner."

Rancho he assumed his country-squire duties with all his old-time vigor. If there were times when he yearned to unleash the hate inside him he never expressed it. If ever in his life he was thoughtful of others, kind, and filled with the tide of human goodness, it was now. If at nights the ghosts of his dead tormented him it was his secret.

"I want to live in peace," he said many times.

He and his men built roads, tilled the fields and found immeasurable solace in honest toil. He insisted that the numerous children around the *rancho* be educated. He spent his own money lavishly, mostly to make others happy.

The Tiger of the North had his fangs removed; on the surface he was harmless. But Mexico is a strange land of exotic broodings. Hates and prejudices linger, seemingly, to eternity — most certainly to the grave. Political treacheries are as recurrent as the tide at Guaymas.

July 20, 1923, Villa, Colonel Trillo and three loyal bodyguards loaded into Pancho's Dodge touring car, and left the ranch to buy supplies in Parral. It was Friday — Villa's unlucky day.

On the outskirts of Parral there is a small bridge. Nearby stands an old 'dobe home. Villa was driving the car as it rattled across the bridge. He was driving slowly. The sun was shining and all the world seemed at peace.

They were only a stone's throw from the roadside house when seven men bolted out the front door. The rifles and pistols in their hands were flaming. Bullets smashed the windshield of the car and ripped into Villa's body. Like a weird automat, he reared up, clutching the steering wheel with one hand and going for his pistol with the other. Other bullets smashed him down.

Villa and his four loyal followers died that day as violently as they had lived. Villa was buried in the cemetery in Parral. Men accused of being the assassins were tried, then released for lack of evidence.

An aging Dorado still lives in Parral. The years have mellowed his erstwhile rapacious instincts. He smiles gently, and his politeness is of the Old World. He has become a star-gazer, a *peon* philosopher, a steady imbiber of *sotol*. He speaks of Villa as if Villa were alive. As the hour grows late, and sleep drugs his eyes, he mumbles profoundly, but sadly.

"Man's body," he says in Spanish, "is inconsequential, but man's soul is infinite." (THE END)

Villa Rides!

9243